ENGINEERED, NOT HOPED FOR.

001 FIRST EDITION

BY ANDRÉ FRANKLIN

ENGINEERED BY DRÉ

engineeredbydre.com · Atlanta, GA

Systems Over Hope. Ownership Over Attention.

First Edition — 2026

Printed in the United States of America

engineeredbydre.com · Atlanta, GA

HOW TO GET THIS BOOK

ENGINEERED, NOT HOPED FOR. is available in four options.

Tier	Price	What's Included
01 — Digital Ebook	$49	Full digital PDF — all 87 chapters Build Checklist — one page, every phase Instant download after purchase
02 — Hard Copy + Ebook	$69	Printed hardcopy — First Edition 2026 Full digital PDF + Build Checklist included Shipped to your door
03 — Full Resource Bundle	$250	Everything in Tier 2 (book + digital PDF) Build Checklist — free with every tier Mockup & Tech Pack templates — all clothing categories Tech Pack Manuscript — how to build & send a tech pack Editable SVG files — all 12 tech pack pages Manufacturer & Contact Directory — 95 vetted contacts
04 — Book + 1-on-1 Consulting	$1,000	Everything in Tier 3 4 dedicated 1-hour calls with André Brand setup, manufacturing, sampling, and launch

Tier 4 consulting calls are 1 hour each. Four calls. Four phases. From zero to selling.

FREE WITH EVERY TIER — BUILD CHECKLIST INCLUDED
Every purchase includes the My Personal Engineered Checklist — one page covering every phase of building a drop. Run through it before every release.

READ BEFORE YOUR FIRST CALL
If you purchased Tier 4, read this entire book before your first consulting call. The calls are built around the framework in these pages. Come to Call 1 having read at least Parts I and II.

TIER 3 TO TIER 4 UPGRADE POLICY
If you previously purchased Tier 3 ($250) and decide to upgrade to Tier 4 ($1,000), your original $250 will be credited — you pay only the difference of $750. Contact shop@engineeredbydre.com with your original order number to apply the credit before purchasing.

This book is for the engineers with a vision bigger than their current reality. For the ones who kept showing up, kept learning, and kept leveling up. If you're willing to stay consistent, you're already ahead of most.

"If you're reading this,
I pray you make it."

— Engineered By Dré

ACKNOWLEDGMENTS

Every brand has a beginning. Mine has a name attached to it.

Hollywood Shack — I would not have started Engineered By Dré without you. Your masterclass on how to start a clothing brand was the spark that lit everything. You gave me the framework. I did the work. But it started with you, and I will never forget that.

To every customer who placed an order, shared a photo, tagged the brand, or told a friend — you are the reason this brand exists at the level it does. Thirty thousand orders. One million dollars in revenue in year one. None of that happens without people who believed before it was obvious to believe.

To the city of Ypsilanti, Michigan — where I was born and raised, where I learned what it means to work for everything you have. That foundation never leaves you.

To Detroit — the city that shaped this brand's identity. The culture, the resilience, the collaborations with the Pistons, the Tigers, the Red Wings. Detroit made Engineered By Dré what it is.

To Atlanta — the city I chose next. Thank you for the energy, the community, and the room to grow.

And to everyone who told me it was not possible — thank you too. Doubt is a powerful motivator when you know how to use it.

— André Franklin

Atlanta, GA · 2026

TABLE OF CONTENTS

INTRODUCTION

Why I Made This Book

I made this book because everywhere I go, people ask me the same questions. In airports while traveling, at pop-ups and events, through direct messages, and in everyday conversations, I constantly hear the same things.

How did you start? How did you find manufacturers? How did you scale? How do you know what to drop next? How do you not quit when it gets hard?

For a long time, I answered these questions one conversation at a time. Eventually, I realized something: when thousands of people are asking the same questions, the answers deserve structure.

This book exists to compile everything I have learned building Engineered By Dré from an idea into a real brand built for longevity. Not theory. Not hype. Real decisions made under real pressure.

I did not write this to flex success. I wrote this to shorten someone else's learning curve. If this book saves you time, money, or mistakes, then it did exactly what it was meant to do.

How This Brand Was Engineered

Engineered By Dré exists because I understood early on that engineering and fashion are not opposites — they are built on the same principles.

I studied Mechanical Engineering at Eastern Michigan University. Engineering taught me how to think in systems: dimensioning, materials, sustainability, and continuous improvement. Fashion uses those same concepts, just applied differently.

Engineering Principle	Fashion Application
Dimensioning	Fit
Material Science	Fabric Selection
Manufacturing	Construction
Sustainability	Longevity

The idea for Engineered By Dré came to me in December 2022. At the time, it only existed in my head. In January 2023, during my senior year of college, I decided to act on it.

At that point, I was a full-time student, working full-time, and building a brand at night. Most of my progress happened after hours, communicating with overseas manufacturers in China while the rest of the world slept.

By March 2023, I officially launched my first products. Within the first three months of business, Engineered By Dré scaled from zero to six figures. By the end of the first year, the brand generated over one million dollars in revenue.

While all of this was happening, I graduated college and began working as an engineer at General Motors. I started operations from my home, then moved into my garage, then a plaza, and eventually a full-size commercial warehouse.

- 30,000+ Orders completed worldwide
- $1M+ Revenue in year one
- 2 Years from idea to global brand

Along the way, collaborations with Wingstop, the Detroit Pistons, Detroit Tigers, and Detroit Red Wings followed. The brand is now recognized globally — even copied by companies like SHEIN and Fashion Nova.

That does not happen by accident. It happens when vision meets discipline, when pressure meets preparation, and when systems replace hope.

"I ONLY WANT TO WORK WITH FRIENDS" was never supposed to be the foundation of the brand. It emerged by listening. Customers repeated it, believed in it, and embodied it. That is what real branding looks like.

PART I — ENGINEERING THE MINDSET

How to think before you build.

CHAPTER 1 — Engineered, Not Hoped For

Most brands do not fail because of a lack of talent. They fail because they were built on hope.

Hope is emotional. Systems are repeatable. A brand that lasts is engineered through structure.

Hope that sales increase. Hope that content goes viral. Hope that the manufacturer cares. Hope that customers come back. Hope feels good — but it is unreliable. Systems are what last.

If success disappears when motivation disappears, it was never engineered. Longevity is built through decisions you can repeat under pressure.

What 'Engineered' Actually Means

Engineering a brand means every decision has a reason. Your pricing is intentional. Your manufacturing process is documented. Your marketing plan repeats. Your identity stays consistent even when trends change.

Engineered brands outlast trend-based brands because their foundation is logic, not luck. When one strategy stops working, the structure allows you to pivot without losing the brand itself.

The Lesson

If something cannot be repeated without stress, it is not a system. Build decisions that work at 2 AM and under deadline.

Motivation

You are not building for one good launch. You are building for years of consistency. Engineer it.

CHAPTER 2 — Move Like You Are Great

"Move like you're great now, and don't wait for people to catch on."

The most important mindset shift you will make as a creator is this: move like the version of yourself you are becoming, not the version you are today. This is not about pretending. This is not about ego. This is about preparation.

Pros of Moving Like Your Future Self	Cons You Must Be Ready For
Builds trust faster	You will outgrow your comfort zone quickly
Attracts aligned customers	You must level up before you feel ready
Makes decision-making clearer	You cannot hide behind excuses
Forces long-term thinking	You will be held to a higher standard
Positions your brand early	Growth demands discomfort

The Lesson

Do not wait for people to catch on. Align your actions with your vision now.

Motivation

Move like that version today. Not tomorrow. Not after validation. Now.

CHAPTER 3 — Data Over Emotion

Sales tell you what sold. Data tells you who bought, why they bought, and what they did next. If you skip this step and rush into selling, you are building blind.

What Data Actually Matters

- What sizes sell the most
- What colors perform best
- Which products sell repeatedly vs. just launch well
- Where your customers are located
- What content leads directly to purchases
- First-time buyers vs. repeat buyers
- Return and exchange reasons
- Where customers drop off during checkout

The Lesson

If you are guessing, you are overpaying somewhere. Data replaces doubt with direction.

Motivation

Brands that last listen before they create again.

CHAPTER 4 — You Do Not Need Permission to Start

One of the biggest reasons creators never begin is because they are waiting to feel ready. Ready with a full plan. Ready with every answer. Ready with perfection. That moment never comes.

Starting creates clarity. Clarity creates direction. Direction creates confidence. You do not learn by thinking. You learn by doing.

The Lesson

Starting imperfectly beats planning perfectly. You can refine a moving system. You cannot refine something that does not exist.

Motivation

Every creator you admire started without a full blueprint. Start now. Perfect later.

CHAPTER 5 — You Are Not Starting From Zero

One of the biggest lies creators tell themselves is that they are starting from nothing. No experience. No advantage. No relevant background. That belief is false.

You are not starting from zero. You are starting from experience. Every job you have worked, every life experience you have lived, every hobby you have spent time on, and every environment you have been shaped by has trained the way you think. That thinking becomes your edge when building a brand.

The Lesson

Stop disqualifying yourself before you begin. You do not need to become someone else to succeed.

Motivation

You are not behind. You are not late. You are prepared in ways you may not recognize yet.

CHAPTER 6 — Get Around People Who Are Doing Better Than You

Your environment is either pulling you forward or holding you back. There is no neutral. The people you spend the most time with shape your ceiling — what you think is possible, what you think is normal, and what you think you deserve.

If everyone around you is operating at the same level you are, nobody in that circle is challenging you to grow. That is comfortable. Comfortable is dangerous.

Getting around people who are doing better than you is not about abandoning where you came from. It is about expanding what you can see. When you are around people who have already solved the problems you are currently stuck on, your timeline shortens. Their lessons become your shortcuts. Their networks become accessible to you. Their standards raise yours just by proximity.

How to Get in the Room

- Attend industry events, trade shows, and pop-ups where operators gather
- Invest in masterminds, courses, or programs where the other participants are ahead of you
- Follow and engage genuinely with builders you respect — real relationships start online
- Offer value before you ask for anything — help, share, support, then connect
- Be willing to be the least experienced person in the room and stay anyway

The room that intimidates you is the room you need to be in. The discomfort you feel around people who are further along is your growth talking. Listen to it.

You become the average of your environment over time. Build the environment intentionally. The people you choose to be around are one of the most important business decisions you will ever make — even if it never shows up in a spreadsheet.

The Lesson

Your network is not just who you know. It is who you are becoming by being around them. Upgrade the room and the room will upgrade you.

Motivation

Find the people who are already where you want to be. Get close. Pay attention. Add value. Grow.

CHAPTER 7 — Comfortable Is a Silent Killer

Comfort feels like safety. It is not. Comfort is the place where brands stop growing, where owners stop learning, and where the distance between you and your competition quietly closes.

The most dangerous moment in any brand's journey is not failure. Failure is loud. You feel it. You respond to it. The most dangerous moment is when things are good enough — when revenue is stable, when the process is familiar, when nothing is urgently wrong. That is when most people stop pushing. And that is exactly when the best brands accelerate.

What Comfort Looks Like in Business

- Running the same ads that worked six months ago without testing new creative
- Working with the same manufacturer without ever pushing for better quality or pricing
- Posting content on the same schedule with the same format because it is familiar
- Avoiding a difficult conversation with a partner, supplier, or customer because it is uncomfortable
- Staying in a market you understand instead of expanding into one you do not

- Not raising prices because you are afraid of the reaction

Every one of those comfort zones is a ceiling. And ceilings are invisible until you hit them.

Be Comfortable Being Uncomfortable

The skill that separates great operators from average ones is not talent. It is the ability to make decisions that are in their best interest even when those decisions are uncomfortable. Letting go of a manufacturer who is not meeting your standards — uncomfortable. Raising prices on a product that is selling — uncomfortable. Investing in a tool or system before you feel financially ready — uncomfortable. Saying no to an opportunity that does not align with your brand — uncomfortable.

Every significant growth moment in business requires you to do something that does not feel good yet. The discomfort is not a warning sign. It is a marker. It means you are at the edge of where you have been before. That edge is exactly where you need to go.

Train yourself to move toward the uncomfortable decision, not away from it. That is the practice. Not once. Every time.

The Lesson

Comfort is not your reward. It is your warning. When everything feels easy, something is not growing.

Motivation

Make the uncomfortable decision. Do it before you feel ready. That is where your next level lives.

CHAPTER 8 — The Long Way Is the Shortcut

Everyone wants results fast. Fast launch. Fast growth. Fast money. And the internet makes it look like that is how it actually works — the overnight success, the viral moment, the brand that blew up in six months.

What you do not see is the two years before the six months. The failed samples. The manufacturers who disappeared. The drops that did not sell. The slow seasons that tested whether this was real or just a phase. The nights of second-guessing. The mornings of starting again anyway.

The people who get to the top quickly rarely stay there. Speed without foundation is just a faster way to fall. The brands that last are the ones that built slowly enough to build correctly.

Why the Long Way Works

When you take the long way — when you learn manufacturing by doing it wrong first, when you build your audience one post at a time, when you develop your eye for quality through sampling and revising — you accumulate something that shortcuts cannot give you: depth.

Depth is what makes you hard to copy. Anyone can launch a brand. Not everyone can sustain one through adversity, adapt through market shifts, and rebuild after setbacks without losing the identity of what they started. That capability only comes from having lived through the slow build.

The person who gets to a certain level too quickly often does not have the endurance to stay there. They built momentum without building the systems underneath it. When the momentum slows — and it always does — there is nothing holding it up.

What the Long Way Actually Teaches You

- How to make decisions under pressure without panicking
- What your customers actually want versus what you think they want
- Which of your instincts to trust and which ones to question
- How to rebuild after something does not work without losing belief
- How to lead the brand when no one is watching and nothing is exciting

Those lessons are not available in a course. They are not in a YouTube video. They come from the long way. And they are what make everything that follows more sustainable.

The Lesson

The shortcut that skips the foundation eventually leads back to it. Build the foundation first. Everything else becomes easier.

Motivation

Trust the slow. The long way is the shortcut. The brands that endure are the ones that refused to rush.

CHAPTER 9 — A Focused Fool Beats a Distracted Genius

Talent is not rare. Focus is.

Look around at the people in your industry who have the most potential. The ones with the sharpest eye for design, the strongest creative instinct, the most natural ability to connect with an audience. Now look at how many of them are actually winning. The gap between those two groups is almost never talent. It is focus.

A focused fool — someone with average ability who locks in on one thing and executes it repeatedly without distraction — will outperform a distracted genius almost every single time. Because results come from repetition and execution, not from potential.

What Distraction Looks Like for Brand Builders

- Starting a second brand before the first one has real traction
- Chasing every new platform as soon as it trends
- Changing the brand direction every time something is not working

- Trying to sell ten products before mastering one
- Watching what competitors are doing instead of building what customers need
- Spending more time consuming content about building than actually building

Distraction feels productive. That is what makes it dangerous. You are busy. You are learning. You are engaged. But nothing is actually moving forward because your attention is fractured across too many things at once.

What Focus Actually Requires

Focus is not just cutting out distractions. It is making a decision about what matters most right now and protecting that decision from everything else that wants your attention. One product. One platform. One marketing channel. One manufacturer relationship. Master it before you add the next one.

The most successful brand operators I have observed are not the most talented. They are the most consistent. They show up to the same thing every day, make it slightly better, and do not let the noise of what everyone else is doing pull them off course. That consistency, compounded over time, creates results that look like talent from the outside.

You do not need to be the smartest person in the room. You need to be the most focused. That is a choice, not a gift.

The Lesson

Potential without focus is just a good story about what could have been. Focus turns average ability into extraordinary results.

Motivation

Pick your lane. Stay in it. Execute relentlessly. The focused fool wins every time.

PART II — STARTING THE BRAND

How to control what you sell.

CHAPTER 10 — Identity Before Product

Most people start brands backward. They design a product first, then try to figure out what the brand is later. That approach creates confusion, inconsistency, and burnout. A product can sell once. A brand is what sells again and again.

The Questions That Come First

- Who is this brand for?
- What does this brand represent?
- Why should someone believe in this brand long term?
- What feeling should people associate with it without explanation?

Rememberable	Recognizable
People recall it without effort	People know it is yours immediately
It creates an impression or emotion	Even without reading the name
It stays in someone's mind when not shopping	Even from a distance or quick glance

---

The Lesson

Identity is not something you figure out later. It is something you commit to early. When identity is clear, the product becomes inevitable.

Motivation

You are ahead if you are building with intention.

CHAPTER 11 — Choosing the Brand Name & Logo

Your brand name and logo are not separate decisions. They are two parts of the same system. The name creates the idea. The logo gives the idea a shape.

Logos can change. Brand names should not. Changing a logo refreshes perception. Changing a brand name resets trust.

Designing With Longevity in Mind

- Your logo must work on tags, packaging, hardware, websites, and garments

- Simple logos scale — complex logos limit growth
- If you are afraid to place your logo prominently, the identity is not fully developed
- Overdesigned logos feel impressive early but become restrictive later

---

The Lesson

Your brand name sets the vision. Your logo expresses it. Strong brands are built by consistency with improvement.

Motivation

Choose a name you can stand behind long term. Design a logo that can evolve without losing identity.

CHAPTER 12 — Choosing the First Product

Your first product is not about following what everyone else is doing. It is about solving a problem you personally understand.

When I started Engineered By Dré, I created something I wanted more of. That is why my first product was the workshirt. I understood the gap. I understood the fit. I understood how I wanted it to function in real life. That clarity mattered more than trends.

The Lesson

Your first product should teach you something. Create what you believe in. Learn deeply. Expand intentionally.

Motivation

Do not be afraid of difficulty. The hard work you do early compounds later.

CHAPTER 13 — Pricing for Longevity

Pricing is not about what you think customers will tolerate. It is about what your business needs to survive.

What Pricing Must Cover

- Manufacturing costs + sampling mistakes
- Shipping, logistics, and packaging
- Marketing, ads, and platform fees
- Returns and exchanges
- Time delays and cash flow gaps
- Growth, reinvestment, and future development

Cheap prices attract short-term customers. Correct pricing attracts aligned customers who respect quality. Pricing teaches customers how to see your brand.

The Lesson

Margin is not greed. Margin is protection. Price so you can still be here next year.

Motivation

A brand that lasts is priced to endure.

CHAPTER 14 — Legitimacy Builds Trust

Legitimacy is not paperwork. Legitimacy is confidence. Customers do not consciously analyze whether your business is legitimate — they feel it.

The Foundation You Cannot Skip

- LLC or equivalent business entity
- EIN (Employer Identification Number)
- Business bank account (separate from personal)
- Clean bookkeeping from day one
- Sales tax awareness
- Clear website policies and contact info

Website Legitimacy Converts Sales

Your website is your storefront. Customers make buying decisions in seconds based on how professional it looks and feels. Clear product descriptions, accurate size charts, visible shipping timelines, return and exchange policies, and terms of service — these are not optional. They are conversion tools.

When I built out the full policy infrastructure for Engineered By Dré — Privacy Policy, Terms of Service, Return & Exchange Policy, Shipping Policy, and a dedicated Contact page — I did not just do it for legal protection. I did it because trust converts. A customer who can find your return policy in seconds is less likely to hesitate at checkout.

Store Features That Reduce Hesitation and Increase Revenue

Beyond policies, the tools you install on your store directly impact how many visitors become buyers. Back in Stock notifications capture demand for sold-out products — instead of losing that customer forever, you keep them in your pipeline. Price drop alerts bring hesitant buyers back when conditions change. Cross-sell and upsell tools — showing related products or accessories — increase average order value without requiring more ad spend.

These are not gimmicks. They are systems. A store without these features is leaving money on the table every single day.

The Lesson

Legitimacy is invisible when done right and painfully obvious when done wrong.

Motivation

Build your brand like it is going to succeed, even before it does.

CHAPTER 15 — What You Need to Start — The Real Startup List

Before the first product ships, before the first manufacturer is contacted, before the first drop is announced — there is a set of tools, equipment, and resources that every brand owner needs to operate. Most people underestimate what it actually takes to get started and then get caught off guard by the expenses that come up repeatedly throughout the life of the business.

This chapter is the honest list. Not just what you need once — but what you will keep spending money on as long as you are running a brand. Understanding these costs upfront means you can plan for them, budget for them, and treat them as the business infrastructure they are rather than surprise expenses that drain your cash.

Design — How You Create What You Sell

Before anything gets manufactured, it has to be designed. Your ability to communicate what you want to a manufacturer visually — through mockups, sketches, or tech packs — determines the quality of what comes back. Invest in design tools early.

Tool	What It's For	Cost	Level
Canva Pro	Quick mockups, social media assets, hang tag design, basic branding	$13/month	Beginner — start here
Adobe Illustrator	Vector logos, tech packs, scalable design files for manufacturers	$22/month (Creative Cloud)	Intermediate — essential at scale
Adobe Photoshop	Photo-realistic mockups, product photography editing, retouching	$22/month (Creative Cloud)	Intermediate
Adobe Creative Cloud	Full suite — Illustrator, Photoshop, InDesign, Premiere	$55/month	Advanced — worth it when you use multiple tools
Procreate (iPad)	Sketching, ideation, on-the-go design concepts	$12.99 one-time	Great for creative ideation

Tool	What It's For	Cost	Level
Figma	UI/web design, mood boards, collaborative design	Free tier available	Useful for website mockups and presentations

Start with Canva for the basics. Add Illustrator when you are communicating with manufacturers — vector files are the standard. Add Photoshop when your product photography needs professional editing. Do not buy the full Creative Cloud suite until you are actively using more than two tools regularly.

Design is a recurring expense. Budget for it monthly from day one. It is not optional — every mockup you send to a manufacturer, every graphic on your website, every piece of content you create requires some form of design tool.

Hardware — The Equipment That Runs the Operation

Your hardware is your production infrastructure. Cheap hardware costs you time and credibility. Invest in tools that will last and perform under the demands of a real business operation.

Equipment	What It's For	Recommended Spec / Notes
Laptop — MacBook Pro or equivalent	Everything — design, communication, Shopify, Klaviyo, ad management	M2 or M3 chip minimum — 16GB RAM — do not cheap out here
iPad (with Apple Pencil)	Sketching in Procreate, signing documents, mobile Shopify management	iPad Pro or Air — pairs with Procreate for design
Label printer — Rollo or DYMO 4XL	Printing shipping labels — essential if you are fulfilling orders yourself	Thermal label printer — no ink costs, fast, clean labels
Thermal label paper / rolls	Consumable for label printer — runs out regularly	Buy in bulk — cheaper per roll and you will always need them
Scale — postal scale	Weighing packages for accurate shipping rates	Any accurate digital scale rated to at least 50 lbs
iPhone or high-quality camera	Product photography, content creation, behind the scenes	Modern iPhone shoots professional quality — upgrade when needed
Ring light or lighting setup	Consistent lighting for product photos and video content	Invest in at least one good light — lighting is everything in photography

Equipment	What It's For	Recommended Spec / Notes
External hard drive or cloud storage	Backing up design files, photos, product assets	2TB minimum — Google Drive or iCloud also essential

The laptop is non-negotiable. Everything your brand does runs through it. A slow, underpowered laptop costs you hours every week in lag, crashes, and frustration. A MacBook Pro with an M-series chip will handle design software, video editing, Shopify admin, and email management simultaneously without breaking a sweat. Buy it once and use it for years.

The label printer is one of the most underrated investments for a brand fulfilling its own orders. A Rollo or DYMO 4XL thermal printer eliminates ink costs entirely, prints labels in seconds, and integrates directly with Shopify Shipping. If you are printing labels from a regular inkjet printer, you are wasting time and money every single day.

Fulfillment Supplies — What You Need to Ship Every Order

These are the consumables that run out regularly and need to be restocked consistently. Budget for them monthly — they are a cost of doing business, not a surprise.

Supply	What It's For	Where to Source	Buy In
Poly mailer bags	Shipping garments — lightweight, waterproof, professional	Uline, Amazon, Alibaba for branded	Bulk — 500 minimum
Branded poly bags (for inside packaging)	The bag the customer sees when they open — your brand on it	Alibaba for custom printed	500–1,000 minimum
Tissue paper	Wrapping product inside the mailer — elevates the experience	Uline, Alibaba, noissue for branded	500 sheets minimum
Shipping tape	Sealing boxes and poly mailers	Uline in bulk rolls	Bulk — runs out fast
Boxes (various sizes)	For orders that need box packaging — higher ticket items	Uline, Packlane for custom branded	Size variety on hand
Stickers	Brand stickers in every order — free marketing with every package	Sticker Mule, StickerGiant	500 minimum

Supply	What It's For	Where to Source	Buy In
Hang tags	Attached to every garment — brand identity on the product	Alibaba, local print shop	500–1,000 minimum
Thank you cards	Personal touch in every package	Vistaprint, Moo, local print	500 minimum
Rubber bands / clips	Keeping folded garments neat	Any office supply store	Small quantity
Packing tissue / filler	Filling space in boxes, protecting product during shipping	Uline, Amazon	As needed

Office Supplies — The Boring Stuff That Keeps the Business Running

These are the unglamorous necessities that every business needs and most brand owners forget to budget for until they run out at the worst possible time.

- Printer and ink (for non-label documents) — contracts, invoices, receipts, customs forms for international orders
- Paper — always running low when you need it most
- Pens, markers, scissors — for labeling, writing notes, cutting samples
- Filing system or folders — keeping physical documents organized: manufacturer contracts, shipping receipts, tax documents
- External monitor — if you are designing for hours daily, a second screen dramatically increases productivity
- Ergonomic chair and desk — you will spend more time at your desk than you expect. Your body will feel it.
- Phone stand or tripod — for filming content, product photos, and video calls with manufacturers
- USB hub / dongles — MacBooks have limited ports — adapters for SD cards, USB drives, external drives are essential

Software and Subscriptions — Your Monthly Business Infrastructure

These are recurring costs that keep the business operating. Most of them are essential. Know what you are paying for and why.

Subscription	Monthly Cost (approx)	What It Does
Shopify Basic	$39/month	Your store — non-negotiable

Subscription	Monthly Cost (approx)	What It Does
Klaviyo	Free up to 250 contacts, then scales	Email marketing — essential
Postscript	Starts around $25/month	SMS marketing
Adobe Creative Cloud	$55/month	Design tools
Canva Pro	$13/month	Quick design and social assets
Zoom	$16/month (Pro)	Manufacturer calls, consulting calls
Google Workspace	$6/month	Professional email, Drive storage
QuickBooks or Wave	$30/month or free	Bookkeeping and financials
Calendly Standard	$10/month	Scheduling consulting calls
Meta Ads	Variable — your ad budget	Paid advertising
Domain name	$12–$20/year	Your website URL
VPN service	$3–$10/month	Security — especially when traveling

Add these up. At minimum, your base software infrastructure costs $150–$200 per month before any ad spend. That is your cost of having a real, operational brand with professional tools. Budget for it. Do not be surprised by it.

Manufacturing Startup Costs — What to Expect Before the First Order

Before any product ships to customers, money goes out the door for development. These are not waste — they are investment. But understanding them upfront prevents the sticker shock that stops many brand owners before they ever launch.

Cost	Approximate Range	Notes
Sample cost (per style)	$100–$400	Non-negotiable — never skip sampling
Shipping from manufacturer for sample	$30–$80 (DHL/FedEx express)	Express shipping — weeks of waiting is not acceptable for samples
Revision sample (if needed)	$100–$400 again	First sample is rarely perfect — budget for at least one revision
Tech pack creation (if outsourced)	$50–$200	Or create yourself with Illustrator — saves money

Cost	Approximate Range	Notes
Bulk order deposit (30% of total)	Varies — depends on order size	Typically 30% upfront, 70% before shipment
Bulk order shipping (sea freight)	$300–$1,500+	Depends on volume and destination
Custom labels and tags for bulk order	$100–$300	Neck labels, hang tags, care labels for the full run
Import duties / customs	Varies — typically 10–30% of product value	Research your product's HTS code and applicable duty rate

The most important number here is the sample cost. Most first-time brand owners budget for one sample and are shocked when the first sample needs revisions. Budget for two samples of every new style — one initial, one revision. If the first sample is perfect, you have money left over. If it needs work, you are prepared.

The Real First-Year Cost Picture

Here is what a realistic first year of building a brand from scratch actually costs — not the minimum fantasy, but a real operational budget:

Category	Year 1 Estimate
LLC formation and EIN	$50–$500 depending on state
Website and domain (Shopify + domain)	$500–$600
Design software (Adobe CC)	$660/year
Laptop (if new)	$1,500–$2,500
Label printer (Rollo)	$100–$150
Sampling (2 styles, 2 samples each)	$800–$3,200
First bulk order (small run)	$2,000–$8,000+
Fulfillment supplies (bags, tissue, tags, stickers)	$400–$800
Marketing and ads (first 6 months)	$1,000–$5,000
Klaviyo, Postscript, apps	$500–$1,200
Photography	$500–$2,000
Miscellaneous (office supplies, shipping, fees)	$500–$1,000
TOTAL ESTIMATE	$8,510–$25,650+

That range is wide because every brand starts differently. Some start with blanks and at-home production — much lower cost. Some go straight to custom manufacturing — higher cost. The point is not to intimidate — it is to inform. Building a real brand costs real money. Most of it comes back when the product sells. But the upfront investment is real and pretending otherwise sets people up for financial shock.

Know the costs. Plan for them. And remember — every one of these expenses is a tax deduction.

The Lesson

The brands that launch prepared outlast the brands that launch unprepared every time. Know what you need. Budget for it. Buy the right tools once instead of the wrong tools twice.

Motivation

This is not a hobby budget. It is a business budget. Treat it that way from the first dollar you spend and every dollar that follows will work harder.

PART III — MANUFACTURING & OWNERSHIP

How to control your supply chain.

CHAPTER 16 — Manufacturing Foundations

Manufacturing Is a Relationship, Not a Transaction

Many creators approach manufacturers looking for the cheapest option. That mindset usually produces average results and long-term frustration. Manufacturers are businesses. If you approach manufacturing focused on clarity, standards, and long-term partnership, the outcome changes.

Control Starts With Clarity

If you want a heavyweight hoodie, specify the exact GSM. If you want premium stitching, request it directly. If you want a specific fabric feel, describe it clearly. If you do not define quality, price will decide for you.

The Lesson

Control outlasts speed.

Motivation

The more you understand this process, the more power you have.

CHAPTER 17 — Finding Manufacturers the Right Way

Platforms like Alibaba are powerful if used correctly and costly if used blindly. Do not search for a product — search for capability. Always ask for real work — photos of previous orders, close-up shots of stitching, real production images.

Signs of a stronger manufacturer: multiple years of operation, verified status, clear communication, willingness to answer detailed questions. A red flag: any manufacturer that immediately pushes price without asking about quality.

The Lesson

Control outlasts speed.

Motivation

The more you understand this process, the more power you have.

CHAPTER 18 — China vs Pakistan Manufacturing

China	Pakistan
Flexibility, customization, quality control	Lower costs, simpler production
Wide range of fabrics and advanced construction	Good for basics: t-shirts, hoodies, fleece
Rewards preparation	Requires closer oversight
Better for complex designs	Better for high-volume basics

No matter where you manufacture, quality does not happen automatically. Location does not determine quality. Clarity does.

The Lesson

Control outlasts speed.

Motivation

The more you understand this process, the more power you have.

CHAPTER 19 — USA vs Overseas Manufacturing

USA Manufacturing	Overseas Manufacturing
Speed, accessibility, tighter control	Lower costs, broader customization
Higher cost, higher minimums	Longer lead times
Best for small runs or premium pricing	Best for scaling
Rewards speed-to-market	Rewards preparation

The Lesson

Control outlasts speed.

Motivation

The more you understand this process, the more power you have.

CHAPTER 20 — At-Home Manufacturing & Using Blanks

Most creators begin by sourcing blank garments from wholesale suppliers (Shaka Wear, Superline Wholesale), then applying designs using heat transfer vinyl, screen printing, direct-to-film transfers, or embroidery. Use this phase to prepare for the next one.

The Lesson

Control outlasts speed.

Motivation

The more you understand this process, the more power you have.

CHAPTER 21 — Mockups & Tech Packs

A mockup shows the product before it exists. A tech pack includes measurements, fabric type, stitching details, branding elements, color codes, and construction notes. Never sample without a mockup. Mockups reduce back and forth, shorten timelines, and protect your budget.

The Lesson

Control outlasts speed.

Motivation

The more you understand this process, the more power you have.

CHAPTER 22 — Samples, Lead Times & Planning Ahead

Samples allow you to test fit, confirm fabric quality, review construction, verify branding placement, and catch mistakes early. Stay involved while the sample is being made. Holiday drops require planning months ahead.

The Lesson

Control outlasts speed.

Motivation

The more you understand this process, the more power you have.

CHAPTER 23 — Fabrics & Material Control

GSM (grams per square meter) tells you how heavy or dense a fabric is. A hoodie around 280 GSM feels lightweight. Around 400 GSM feels heavier and more substantial — that weight communicates quality before a customer ever sees the price. If you want premium, you must request premium.

The Lesson

Control outlasts speed.

Motivation

> **Tier 3 Bundle — The exact resources mentioned in this chapter are included.**
> *Your bundle includes ready-to-use tech pack templates (editable SVGs for Illustrator), a full Tech Pack Manuscript walking through every section, and a Manufacturer Directory with 95 contacts across 27 categories.*

CHAPTER 24 — References, Size Charts & Fit Consistency

Start with a garment you already love. Send it to your manufacturer as a reference. Measure one size you already trust and instruct them to grade all other sizes from that base. Fit becomes part of your brand identity.

The Lesson

Control outlasts speed.

Motivation

The more you understand this process, the more power you have.

CHAPTER 25 — Molding Your Manufacturer

Molding a manufacturer means training them to understand your expectations and execute consistently at your level. If stitching is sloppy, call it out. If fabric feels wrong, stop production. Quality is a conversation, not a one-time request.

The Lesson

Control outlasts speed.

Motivation

The more you understand this process, the more power you have.

CHAPTER 26 — Preorders, Bulk Orders & Ready to Ship

A preorder means you sell before you produce. Bulk is about how you manufacture — placing a large production order after demand is proven. The transition from preorder to ready-to-ship should be data-driven, not emotional.

The Lesson

Control outlasts speed.

Motivation

The more you understand this process, the more power you have.

CHAPTER 27 — High-Risk Orders & Ownership

Preorders allow you to test real demand, fund production with customer money, and reduce unsold inventory. If the order is high-risk, the money should stay with you. Smart control outlasts fast growth.

The Lesson

Control outlasts speed.

Motivation

The more you understand this process, the more power you have.

PART IV — ADVERTISING, BRANDING & ATTENTION

How trust turns into revenue.

CHAPTER 28 — Turning Viewers Into Buyers (The Trust Stack)

Views do not equal sales. Trust does. A brand can have thousands of views and still struggle to convert if trust is missing. Attention is temporary. Trust compounds.

Your job is not to convince. Your job is to remove hesitation. Hesitation usually comes from unclear sizing, weak visuals, inconsistent branding, and missing information. When those gaps are removed, conversion improves naturally.

The Lesson

Control outlasts speed.

Motivation

Build rooms. Control access. Let belief do the selling.

CHAPTER 29 — Data Over Emotion in Marketing

Track which sizes and colors sell most. Track what content leads to purchases. Track which ads convert — not just which get views. Track retention and lifetime value. Data should guide design, not restrict creativity.

The Lesson

Control outlasts speed.

Motivation

Build rooms. Control access. Let belief do the selling.

CHAPTER 30 — The Double R Method

Every design must pass two tests: Rememberable and Recognizable. Rememberable means people recall it without effort. Recognizable means people know it is yours immediately, even without seeing your name. If your design could belong to anyone, it belongs to no one.

The Lesson

Control outlasts speed.

Motivation

Build rooms. Control access. Let belief do the selling.

CHAPTER 31 — Branding Down to the Details

Branding does not stop at the garment. Real branding lives in the details customers interact with after the purchase. Neck tags, packaging, labels, rivets, buttons, metal hardware, hang tags — every touchpoint reinforces identity. I engrave a gear into every button. Details communicate intention.

The Lesson

Control outlasts speed.

Motivation

Build rooms. Control access. Let belief do the selling.

CHAPTER 32 — Create the Room Your Product Lives In

Most brands focus only on the product. Great brands design the environment around the product. I create cover art for everything I sell because perception forms before inspection. The room includes product photography, cover art, website layout, launch visuals, copy and storytelling, and rollout timing.

The Lesson

Control outlasts speed.

Motivation

Build rooms. Control access. Let belief do the selling.

CHAPTER 33 — Iconic Marketing Creates Belief

Iconic marketing does not explain. It makes people believe. Marketing is not promotion. It is positioning. Strong visual identity across every post. Campaigns that feel planned. Messaging that stays consistent. Rollouts that feel like moments, not uploads.

The Lesson

Control outlasts speed.

Motivation

Build rooms. Control access. Let belief do the selling.

CHAPTER 34 — Sell the Brand, Not the Product

Luxury brands do not sell products. They sell belief, identity, and experience. When you sell a product, you must convince someone every time. When you sell a brand, people already believe before they click. A rollout is how you introduce a product to the world — visual direction, location, models, copy, timing, and sequence.

The Lesson

Control outlasts speed.

Motivation

Build rooms. Control access. Let belief do the selling.

CHAPTER 35 — When a Product Is Not Moving

Not every product will sell immediately. Slow movement is not a verdict — it is feedback. One strategy: mark the product as sold out, let time pass, then reintroduce as 'Back In Stock.' Scarcity changes behavior. The same product often performs better the second time because perception changed.

The Lesson

Control outlasts speed.

Motivation

Build rooms. Control access. Let belief do the selling.

CHAPTER 36 — Pivoting Without Panicking

When a product is not moving, your response matters more than the product itself. Panic creates bad decisions. Discipline creates clarity. Do not discount immediately, overexplain to customers, or abandon your brand identity. Instead: reposition, refresh visuals, adjust messaging.

The Lesson

Control outlasts speed.

Motivation

Build rooms. Control access. Let belief do the selling.

CHAPTER 37 — The Private Room vs Public Room

Every strong brand operates in two rooms. The private room is where your core audience lives — email subscribers, SMS subscribers, repeat buyers. They get early access, first information, and priority opportunities. The public room is where discovery happens.

Building Your Private Room With the Right Tools

The tools you use to manage this relationship matter. Email marketing platforms like Klaviyo allow you to segment your audience — people who bought once versus people who buy every drop. SMS platforms like Postscript let you reach customers directly on their phones, which converts at higher rates than email for time-sensitive drops.

The private room is not just a concept — it is a system. Popups that capture email and phone numbers. Flows that automatically send early access notifications. Sequences that build anticipation before a drop opens. These tools work while you sleep.

The Lesson

Control outlasts speed.

Motivation

Build rooms. Control access. Let belief do the selling.

CHAPTER 38 — Early Access, Rollouts & Controlled Demand

Early access should feel like a privilege, not a feature. A strong rollout moves in layers: private room first, public room second. When access feels earned, buying feels urgent.

The Lesson

Control outlasts speed.

Motivation

Build rooms. Control access. Let belief do the selling.

CHAPTER 39 — Running Ads as a System

Most brands do not fail at ads because the product is bad. They fail because they treat ads like a gamble instead of a system. Ads are not luck. Ads are levers. And like any lever, how you position it determines how much it moves.

The Four Levers of a Strong Ad System

Lever	What It Controls	The Rule
TIME	Algorithm learning	Run ads 30+ days before judging results
TARGETING	Who sees the ad	Pay for relevance, not volume
TRAFFIC TEMPERATURE	Stage of the buyer	Cold = discovery, Retargeting = conversion
CREATIVE	What the ad shows	Change one variable at a time

Meta Ads (Facebook & Instagram)

Meta remains the most powerful paid advertising platform for fashion and apparel brands. The algorithm rewards consistency, not spending. Here is how to build it correctly:

- Start with a $10–$20/day budget on a single ad set. Do not spread thin.
- Use broad targeting first — let Meta find your buyer instead of guessing demographics
- Run video or carousel creative showing the product in real environments, not flat lays
- Give the algorithm 1,000 impressions before drawing conclusions
- Retarget website visitors and add-to-cart users with a separate ad set at a higher budget
- Build a lookalike audience from your customer list once you have 500+ purchases

TikTok Ads

TikTok rewards authenticity over production value. What converts on TikTok looks different from Meta. Here is what works:

- Organic-feeling videos outperform polished ads — show the product being worn, unboxed, or styled
- Hook viewers in the first two seconds — the scroll is fast
- Use the Spark Ads feature to boost organic posts that already have traction
- TikTok's algorithm favors content, not targeting — start with broad audiences and let the platform find your buyer
- Test multiple short video creatives — volume of creative testing matters more on TikTok than any other platform

The Retargeting Stack

Cold audiences discover you. Warm audiences buy from you. Most brands spend all their budget on cold traffic and wonder why ads are expensive. The fix: dedicate 30–40% of your ad budget to retargeting — people who visited your site, watched your videos, or added to cart but did not purchase. These people already know you exist. Your job is to remind them and remove the last barrier.

What to Never Do With Ads

- Never run ads to a product page with no reviews, no clear description, and no visible policies
- Never judge an ad campaign in the first seven days — the algorithm is still learning
- Never run the same creative for more than 30 days without refreshing it

- Never increase budget by more than 20% at a time — large increases reset the algorithm's learning
- Never confuse reach with results — impressions mean nothing without conversions

---

The Lesson

Ads stop feeling expensive when they become predictable. Build the system before you scale the spend.

Motivation

The algorithm rewards patience. Every ad campaign you run teaches you something. Pay for the lesson. Apply it.

CHAPTER 40 — Converting Viewers Into Buyers — The Store Infrastructure

Getting traffic to your store is only half the equation. The other half is what happens when a visitor arrives. Most brands lose the sale not because the product is wrong but because the store itself creates friction.

I spent time engineering the infrastructure of engineeredbydre.com the same way I engineer products — intentionally, systematically, and with the goal of removing every reason someone might leave without buying.

The Conversion Stack

These are the layers that turn a store visit into a purchase:

Layer	Tool / Feature	What It Does
Email Capture	Klaviyo Popup (15% OFF)	Captures email before they leave, offers incentive to buy
SMS Capture	Postscript	Builds direct mobile line to your most engaged customers
Back In Stock	Kbite Notify Me	Captures demand for sold-out products, recovers lost sales
Price Drop Alerts	Kbite Price Drop	Brings back hesitant buyers when conditions change
Cross-Sell / Upsell	Zoorix	Shows complementary products at product page and in cart
Recently Viewed	Native Shopify Section	Reduces friction for returning browsers

Layer	Tool / Feature	What It Does
Trust Signals	Policies + Contact Page	Removes hesitation at checkout
Fraud Protection	NoFraud	Protects revenue from chargebacks before they happen

Why Each Layer Matters

Email capture with an incentive is the single most important conversion tool for a fashion brand. Someone who gives you their email is telling you they are interested but not ready. Your job is to stay in front of them until they are ready. A 15% off popup — shown once per visitor, with a teaser tab for returning visitors — keeps the offer available without annoying the customer.

Back In Stock notifications are one of the most underused tools in fashion. When a product sells out, most brands lose that customer permanently. With a notification system, you capture their email or phone number and bring them back the moment inventory returns. That is a customer you already spent money to acquire. It costs nothing extra to recover them.

Cross-sell and upsell tools — showing a customer who is buying a workshirt that wallet chains, beanies, and belts exist — increase average order value without requiring additional ad spend. You are serving the customer and growing the order at the same time.

Fraud protection is the layer most brands skip until it is too late. Chargebacks are not just financial losses — they threaten your payment processor relationship. A fraud review system that screens orders before they ship prevents the chargeback from ever happening, rather than fighting it after the fact.

The Private Room in Practice

Every email and SMS subscriber you capture is a member of your private room. They have opted in. They want to hear from you. A structured email flow — welcome sequence, back in stock alerts, abandoned cart reminders, post-purchase follow-up — runs automatically and generates revenue while you focus on building.

What the Infrastructure Looks Like When It Is Running

- A visitor lands on your site from an ad
- After a few seconds, a popup offers 15% off in exchange for their email
- They browse a workshirt, see a wallet chain recommended in the cross-sell section
- They add both to cart — average order value increases

- They check out — NoFraud reviews the order before it ships
- Three days later, an automated email asks how they are enjoying their purchase
- The workshirt they viewed but didn't buy triggers a price drop alert when it goes on sale
- They come back. They buy again.

This is not theory. This is the infrastructure of a brand that converts and retains.

The Lesson

Traffic without infrastructure is waste. Build the store that converts before you scale the ads that drive traffic.

Motivation

You do not need more visitors. You need a better reason for the ones you have to stay.

CHAPTER 41 — The Three-Piece Puzzle

After years of building, watching other brands grow, and studying what actually separates the brands that convert from the ones that get traffic but stay broke — I keep coming back to the same formula. Three pieces. Every successful brand has all three. Every struggling brand is missing at least one.

Piece 1 — A Great Product

This is where it starts. Not a good product. A great one. A product that does what it promises, looks like it costs more than it does, and makes the person wearing it feel like they made the right decision. A product people talk about without being asked. A product that creates repeat customers because the first experience was that good.

Most brands underinvest here because product development is slow, expensive, and uncertain. They would rather spend on ads and hope the product is good enough. It is not a sustainable strategy. A great product is the only marketing that compounds forever. Every satisfied customer is an ambassador who does not charge a commission.

Ask yourself honestly: Is my product the best version of what it could be right now? If the answer is anything other than yes — that is your first priority. Not the website. Not the content. The product.

Piece 2 — A High-Converting Store

Your store is not just where people buy. It is where people decide whether to believe in you. A high-converting store does not need to be the most beautiful website on the internet. It needs to do one thing extremely well: remove every reason someone might hesitate to buy.

That means product photos that show the item clearly and in context. Descriptions that answer questions before they are asked. Size charts that are accurate. Policies that are visible and clear. Reviews that show real people had a real experience. A checkout process that does not feel risky.

When someone lands on your store, they are making a decision about trust in seconds. Every element of the page either builds that trust or erodes it. Your store should make the visitor feel like buying from you is the obvious choice — not a leap of faith.

- Professional photography — not just flat lays, but worn, in context, and styled
- Clear product descriptions — material, fit, sizing notes, care instructions
- Visible trust signals — reviews, policies, contact info, return window
- Fast load time — slow websites kill conversions before the page even loads
- Mobile-first design — the majority of your traffic is on a phone
- A simple, clean checkout — every extra step loses buyers

Piece 3 — Content That Makes People Feel Something

Content is not posting. Content is communication. The difference between content that gets likes and content that drives purchases is feeling. Does the viewer feel something when they watch it? Do they see themselves in it? Does it create a desire they did not know they had before they hit play?

The best content for a fashion brand does not explain the product. It shows the life the product belongs to. It puts the product in a world — a mood, a moment, an identity — and lets the viewer decide if that world is theirs. When they decide it is, the purchase is almost already made.

Content that impels someone to buy is not about production quality. It is about authenticity and specificity. Raw footage shot on an iPhone of the right moment, in the right location, with the right energy, will outperform a polished ad with no soul every single time. Because people do not buy products. They buy the feeling the product gives them access to.

Content That Gets Scrolled Past	Content That Gets the Click
Generic product flat lay on white background	Product worn in a real, recognizable environment
'New drop available now'	'You've been asking for this — it's here'
Studio-perfect but emotionally flat	Raw, real, and recognizable
Focused on features	Focused on feeling
Tells you what to think	Makes you feel it yourself
Posted on a schedule	Posted when it has something to say

Why All Three Pieces Must Work Together

A great product with a bad store gets traffic that does not convert. A great store with bad content gets no traffic at all. Great content that drives traffic to a bad store is the most frustrating situation of all — you earned the attention and lost the sale.

When all three are aligned — when the product is excellent, the store removes hesitation, and the content creates desire — the business stops feeling like a struggle and starts feeling like a system. Sales become predictable. Repeat customers become frequent. Word of mouth becomes a channel.

Audit yourself right now against the three pieces. Be honest. Not where you want to be — where you actually are. The weakest piece is where your attention belongs next.

The Lesson

You cannot outrun a weak product with strong content. You cannot outrun a weak store with strong ads. All three pieces must be in place. Build them in order. Maintain them together.

Motivation

Great product. High-converting store. Content that makes people feel something. That is the formula. Engineer all three.

CHAPTER 42 — Build for Everyone — The Power of a Versatile Collection

One of the most significant drivers of Engineered By Dré's growth has been something that most brand owners never think to do intentionally: building a collection that serves a genuinely diverse customer base. Men, women, kids. Feminine styles and non-feminine styles. Matching family sets. Outerwear, accessories, and home decor. Not as a gimmick — as a deliberate strategy to expand who the brand belongs to.

Most fashion brands pick a lane and stay in it. Men's streetwear. Women's basics. Kids clothing. And staying in that lane feels safe because it is focused. But focus becomes a ceiling when you realize that the people who love your brand do not exist in only one demographic. They come as couples. They come as families. They come in different expressions of style. When your collection only serves one of them, you leave the rest of their purchasing power on the table.

This chapter is about how to think about collection versatility — not as losing your identity but as expanding who your brand belongs to without diluting what it stands for.

Listen to Your Customer First

The most important thing before expanding your collection in any direction is this: listen before you build. Your customers will tell you exactly what they want if you create the conditions for them to say it.

The DMs asking if you have kids sizes. The comments from women saying they wish the fit was different. The partner of a customer asking where to get the matching piece. The messages asking if you sell anything for the home. These are not random requests

— they are market research happening in real time, for free, directly from people who already trust your brand.

Before you design a new category, look at your existing data. What are your customers asking for that you do not offer? What questions come up repeatedly in your customer service inbox? What do people tag you in that you do not currently sell? The collection expansion that works best is the one the customer is already asking for — not the one the brand owner decides to build on a creative impulse.

- Check your DMs and comments for recurring product requests
- Look at your customer service emails — repeated questions are product gap signals
- Run an Instagram or email survey — ask your audience directly what they want next
- Look at what customers buy together — which products are frequently in the same order?
- Look at who is buying — are there demographics you are not actively designing for but who are purchasing anyway?

Men, Women, and the Non-Binary Shopper

Most streetwear brands start with men's sizing and silhouettes. When women start buying — and they will, because great design does not have a gender — the brand has two choices: ignore it, or respond to it.

Responding to it does not mean creating a separate women's line that waters down the original aesthetic. It means understanding that women who love your brand may want options. Some want the oversized men's fit — they prefer to size down and wear it that way. Others want a silhouette designed for their body. Some want a more feminine expression of the brand. Others want the same streetwear energy, just cut differently.

Offering both is not confusing — it is inclusive. And inclusive brands have larger addressable markets than exclusive ones. The key is that both expressions feel like the same brand. The design language, the quality, the identity — all consistent. The fit and silhouette — adapted for who is wearing it.

Kids Matching the Adults — One of the Highest-Converting Strategies in Fashion

When I introduced kids sizes that matched the adult collection, something happened that I want every brand owner reading this to understand: people bought both. Parents who were already customers bought the adult piece for themselves and the matching piece for their child in the same order. Average order value went up. Customer loyalty went up. The brand became something the whole family wore — not just one person.

That is not a small thing. A brand that a family wears together becomes part of their identity in a way that a single-person brand cannot. It shows up in family photos. In holiday outfits. In the kids' school photos. In content that parents post organically because they are proud of how the family looks together. That content reaches every parent in their network who has kids the same age.

Matching kids and adult pieces also increases the average customer's lifetime value. A parent who buys your adult pieces will come back for kids pieces as the child grows. A size 2T customer becomes a 4T customer, then a youth medium, then eventually an adult customer of their own. You are building a relationship with a family — not just a transaction with one person.

Women's Styles — Feminine and Non-Feminine

Women who shop streetwear and fashion brands exist on a spectrum. Some want traditionally feminine silhouettes — fitted, curved, softer. Others want the same oversized, boxy, streetwear-forward energy as the men's collection. Offering only one of those options means you are designing for half the women who love your brand.

The solution is not creating two entirely separate collections. It is being intentional about offering both expressions within the same aesthetic. A fitted version and an oversized version of the same design. A cropped option alongside a full-length one. The brand identity stays consistent — the options expand who can find themselves in it.

Pay attention to how women are already styling your product. If they are buying men's pieces and wearing them as dresses or oversized fits — that is data. If they are asking for more curve-friendly silhouettes — that is data. Let what customers are already doing with your product guide what you design next.

Outerwear — The Category That Sells Year-Round in Different Markets

Outerwear — jackets, flannels, vests, bombers — is one of the most consistently high-performing categories in independent fashion for several reasons. It is a statement piece. It gets worn over everything else, which means the brand logo and aesthetic gets maximum visibility. It photographs well. And it justifies a higher price point because customers perceive outerwear as a larger purchase that should last.

Outerwear also travels across seasons depending on your market. A heavy flannel that sells as fall-winter outerwear in Michigan sells as a year-round layering piece in warmer climates. A lightweight vest sells in spring and fall. Building a strong outerwear category means having products that move in every market regardless of season.

Accessories — The Highest-Margin, Lowest-Risk Category

Accessories — wallet chains, beanies, bags, belts, keychains, jewelry — are often the highest-margin items in a fashion brand's lineup. The manufacturing cost is lower relative to the retail price, the storage footprint is small, and they purchase at a lower price point which makes them easier for new customers to try the brand for the first time.

Accessories also serve the customer who wants to represent the brand but is not ready to commit to a higher-ticket garment yet. A $35 wallet chain or a $25 beanie is a low-friction entry point. When that customer has a great experience with the accessory —

quality, packaging, delivery — they are primed to trust the brand on the bigger purchase next time.

Cross-selling accessories with garments is one of the easiest ways to increase average order value. A customer buying a workshirt who sees a matching wallet chain in the cart cross-sell section is already in a buying state of mind. The accessory is a natural addition, not a separate purchase decision.

Home Decor — Extending the Brand Into the Customer's Life

Home decor is a category most fashion brands never consider. It is also one of the most powerful ways to deepen the relationship between a brand and its most loyal customers. A customer who wears your brand and has your brand in their home has made you part of their identity in a fundamentally different way than a customer who just owns one piece.

Home decor does not need to be a full furniture line. It can be as focused as a branded candle, a throw blanket, a poster, or a ceramic mug. The design language of the brand applied to objects that live in someone's space. Every time that customer sits in their home and sees something with your brand on it, the relationship reinforces itself.

Home decor also photographs in a way that garments do not. A branded candle on a coffee table in a well-lit room is aspirational content. Customers who style their space with your brand and share it on social media are creating marketing material that reaches their entire following — people who trust their taste and see the brand in a lifestyle context rather than a product context.

The Versatile Collection Framework — How to Think About It

Category	Who It Serves	Why It Works Together
Men's collection	Male customers — core audience for most streetwear brands	Foundation — sets the brand identity
Women's — oversized/streetwear fit	Women who prefer the streetwear silhouette	Same product, same identity — just different sizing
Women's — fitted/feminine	Women who want curve-friendly or softer expressions	Expands the women's market without diluting identity
Kids matching adults	Families — parents who already buy the adult collection	Increases AOV, builds family loyalty, generates organic content
Outerwear	Everyone — high-visibility statement pieces	Elevates perceived brand value, high-margin, year-round
Accessories	Entry-level buyers and existing customers	Low-friction first purchase, high-margin, cross-sell naturally

Category	Who It Serves	Why It Works Together
Home decor	Most loyal customers — brand identity buyers	Deepens relationship, creates lifestyle content, repeat purchase

The Business Case — Why Versatility Increases Revenue

Every category you add that serves an existing customer is revenue that does not require a new customer acquisition cost. The family that shops with you buys more per visit. The customer who wears your brand and decorates with your brand spends more annually. The person who came for a beanie and stayed for the flannel has a higher lifetime value than the person who bought one workshirt and moved on.

A versatile collection also means your brand is relevant in more gifting moments — holidays, birthdays, anniversaries, baby showers. When someone in a customer's life needs a gift and that customer is already a fan of your brand, a versatile collection gives them options that fit the person they are shopping for. That is revenue you earn without spending a dollar on acquisition.

The brand that serves a whole customer — and their family, and their home — is much harder to replace than the brand that serves only one part of who they are.

The Lesson

The biggest mistake in building a collection is designing for an imaginary customer instead of listening to the real one. Your customers will tell you who they are, what they need, and where your brand can go next. Listen. Build. Let the collection evolve the way the brand does — with intention and in response to real demand.

Motivation

Men. Women. Kids. Accessories. Outerwear. Home. When your brand becomes part of a family's identity — not just one person's wardrobe — you have built something that is very difficult to walk away from. That is the kind of loyalty that compounds for years.

CHAPTER 43 — How to Create Content That Actually Converts

Chapter 40 gave you the framework. This chapter gives you the playbook. Because knowing that content matters is not the same as knowing how to make content that works. Most brand owners understand they need to post. Very few understand what to post, how to shoot it, and how to make someone feel something in the first three seconds before they scroll away.

Let us break this down to what actually works.

The Phone Is Enough

The number one excuse brand owners use to avoid creating content is that they do not have a professional camera, a photographer, or a studio. Let that go right now. The iPhone in your pocket has shot content that has generated millions of dollars in revenue for fashion brands. The camera is not the variable. The eye is.

What makes content work is not resolution. It is composition, lighting, and authenticity. Natural light from a window or an open doorway will outperform an expensive ring light in the wrong environment almost every time. A real location — a street corner, a rooftop, a warehouse, a park — will outperform a white studio backdrop for most fashion brands because real locations communicate a lifestyle, and lifestyle is what sells clothes.

- Shoot in natural light whenever possible — golden hour (just after sunrise or just before sunset) is free and cinematic
- Find locations that match the energy of the brand — the setting tells half the story
- Shoot horizontal and vertical — horizontal for website and YouTube, vertical for Reels and TikTok
- Shoot more than you think you need — edit down, never wish you had more
- The best shot is often the one between the posed ones — candid, real, unguarded

Brand Content vs Product Content

There are two types of content every fashion brand needs, and most brands only make one of them.

Brand Content	Product Content
Builds identity and culture	Drives sales and conversion
Shows the world the brand belongs to	Shows the product clearly
Makes people want to be part of something	Makes people want to own something
Does not always feature a product	Always features a product
Builds long-term trust and recognition	Drives short-term action
Examples: behind the scenes, brand story, lifestyle shots	Examples: product reveals, unboxing, styling videos, drop announcements

Brand content fills your feed with identity. Product content fills your register. You need both. The ratio that works for most fashion brands is roughly 60% brand content to 40% product content. When your feed is only product posts, it starts to feel like a catalog. When it is only brand content, people forget you sell something.

The brands that dominate social are the ones that make you fall in love with the world they represent before they ever ask you to buy anything. By the time the product drops, you already want it — because you already want to be part of what the brand represents.

Storytelling in 7 Seconds

On TikTok and Instagram Reels, you have approximately three seconds to stop the scroll and seven seconds to earn the watch. That is it. If the first frame of your video does not create a reason to keep watching, the algorithm buries it and your audience never sees it.

The hook is everything. The hook is the first visual, the first word, or the first action. It answers the subconscious question every viewer is asking the moment they see any piece of content: Why should I keep watching this?

Weak Hook	Strong Hook
'New drop just dropped'	Starting mid-action — someone already wearing the product in a compelling setting
Logo intro or brand name card	A question or statement that creates instant curiosity
Product on a hanger or table	Someone reacting to seeing the product for the first time
'Check out our new collection'	'I spent six months making this and I need you to see it'
Slow pan across folded clothes	Fast cut between multiple colorways with music that matches the energy

After the hook earns the watch, the middle builds desire and the end drives action. The action does not always have to be 'buy now.' It can be 'follow for the drop,' 'comment your size,' or 'save this for when it launches.' The goal is engagement that signals to the algorithm that your content deserves to be shown to more people.

Platform Strategy — What Works Where

Platform	Content Style That Works	Primary Goal	Best For
Instagram Reels	Fast-cut, trend-aware, visually polished	Discovery and brand awareness	Reaching new audiences
Instagram Feed	High-quality editorial, consistent aesthetic	Brand credibility and identity	First impressions and trust
Instagram Stories	Raw, behind the scenes, polls, countdowns	Community and retention	Keeping existing followers engaged
TikTok	Authentic, trend-native, personality-driven	Viral reach and new audience	Growth at scale

Platform	Content Style That Works	Primary Goal	Best For
YouTube Shorts	Process videos, tutorials, brand story	Long-term SEO and trust	People researching the brand
YouTube Long-form	Behind the brand, day in the life, deep dives	Deep brand loyalty	Your most committed audience

You do not need to be on every platform. You need to be excellent on the platforms where your customer already spends time. For most streetwear and fashion brands, Instagram and TikTok are non-negotiable. YouTube is optional but powerful for building long-term brand depth. Start with two platforms. Master them before adding a third.

Content That Uses Your Customers

The most credible content your brand can have is content you did not create — content your customers created. User-generated content (UGC) is the modern version of word of mouth. When real customers post themselves wearing your product, tag your brand, and share their experience, it does something your own content cannot: it proves the product is real, wearable, and worth buying.

- Create a hashtag for your brand and encourage customers to use it
- Repost customer content with credit — it rewards them and provides you with free authentic content
- Feature customer photos on your website homepage and product pages
- Ask for reviews and video testimonials after purchase in your post-purchase email flow
- Run challenges or campaigns that invite customers to create content around your product

The 'Made by us, Shared by you' section on your website serves exactly this purpose. When a potential customer sees real people — not models, not influencers — wearing your product in their real life, the barrier to purchase drops significantly. They stop asking 'Is this worth it?' and start asking 'Which size should I get?'

Staying Consistent Without Burning Out

The number one reason brand owners fall off their content schedule is not laziness. It is that they create content one piece at a time. You cannot sustain that. Sitting down every day trying to come up with something to post is exhausting and inefficient. The solution is batching.

Batching means dedicating one focused block of time to creating multiple pieces of content at once. One good shoot session — two to three hours in the right location with the right outfits — can produce enough content for two to four weeks of posting. One filming session can generate a week of Reels and TikToks. One writing session can produce a week of captions.

Content Batch Session	What It Produces
2-hour photo shoot at one location	15–30 high quality images for feed, stories, and product pages
1-hour video session with 3 outfits	5–10 Reels and TikToks with multiple angles and hooks
30-minute behind the scenes capture	Story content, UGC-style clips, process content
1-hour caption writing session	2 weeks of captions written and ready to schedule
1 drop day documentation	Reveal content, reaction content, packing content, shipping content

When content is batched, it can be scheduled. When it is scheduled, it posts consistently even on days when you are traveling, in production meetings, or simply not in the mood to create. Consistency is what the algorithm rewards. Consistency is what builds an audience. You cannot be consistent when you create one piece at a time.

The Content Calendar

A content calendar does not need to be complicated. It needs to answer one question for every day you plan to post: what goes up and where. A simple week might look like this:

Day	Platform	Content Type	Goal
Monday	Instagram Feed	Editorial product photo	Brand credibility
Tuesday	TikTok + Reels	Behind the scenes — manufacturing or process	Engagement and reach
Wednesday	Instagram Stories	Poll or question — size feedback, color preference	Community and data
Thursday	TikTok + Reels	Styling video — how to wear the product	Conversion intent
Friday	Instagram Feed	Lifestyle photo — product in a real environment	Brand identity
Saturday	Stories + TikTok	Customer repost or UGC feature	Social proof

Day	Platform	Content Type	Goal
Sunday	No post	Plan and batch for the week ahead	Sustainability

This is a framework, not a rule. Adapt it to your brand, your schedule, and your capacity. The goal is to have a plan before the week starts so you are never scrambling to post something just to stay active. Scrambled content shows. Planned content performs.

The Lesson

Content is the invitation. The product is the experience. The store is where the decision gets made. When all three are working, people do not feel sold to — they feel found.

Motivation

You do not need a production budget. You need a phone, a location, a story, and the discipline to show up consistently. That is what builds an audience that buys.

CHAPTER 44 — Wholesale & Consignment — Expanding Beyond Your Website

Most independent fashion brands treat their website as their only sales channel. That is a ceiling most of them never recognize until they hit it. Your website can only reach people who already know you exist or who find you through ads and content. Wholesale and consignment open a completely different door — they put your product in front of people who have never heard of you, in environments they already trust.

These are two of the most underused revenue channels in independent fashion. Used correctly, they can accelerate brand recognition, generate revenue from channels you do not have to manage daily, and legitimize your brand in ways that digital presence alone cannot.

Wholesale — What It Is and How It Works

Wholesale means selling your product to a retailer at a reduced price — typically 50% of your retail price — and the retailer sells it in their store at full retail or above. You get paid when you deliver the order. The retailer takes on the inventory and the responsibility of selling it to their customers.

Example	Your Cost to Make	Your Wholesale Price	Retailer Sells For	Your Profit Per Unit
Workshirt	$35	$75 (50% of $150 retail)	$150	$40 per unit
Hoodie	$45	$90 (50% of $180 retail)	$180	$45 per unit

Example	Your Cost to Make	Your Wholesale Price	Retailer Sells For	Your Profit Per Unit
Beanie	$12	$25 (50% of $50 retail)	$50	$13 per unit

The margin is tighter than direct-to-consumer but the advantages are significant. You move inventory in bulk. You get paid upfront without running ads. You get your product in front of a new audience that the retailer has already built. And being stocked in a real store adds a layer of legitimacy to your brand that online presence alone does not provide.

The Wholesale Pricing Rule

This is the most important thing to understand about wholesale before you ever approach a retailer: your retail price must be built to support a wholesale price. If your product costs $35 to make and you retail it for $75, you cannot wholesale it — there is no margin left after you sell it to the retailer at $37.50.

The formula is simple: your manufacturing cost should be no more than 25–30% of your retail price. If it costs $35 to make, your retail price should be at least $120–$140 to support a healthy wholesale margin. This is why pricing for longevity — covered earlier in this book — is not just about your direct-to-consumer business. It is about keeping every future revenue channel open.

Manufacturing Cost	Minimum Retail Price for Wholesale	Wholesale Price (50%)	Your Margin at Wholesale
$20	$80+	$40	$20 per unit
$35	$140+	$70	$35 per unit
$50	$200+	$100	$50 per unit
$75	$300+	$150	$75 per unit

If your current pricing does not support wholesale, that is data. It means you either need to reduce your manufacturing cost, increase your retail price, or accept that wholesale is not a viable channel at your current price point. Do not force it. Fix the foundation first.

Consignment — What It Is and How It Works

Consignment is a different arrangement. Your product sits in the retailer's store but you retain ownership until it sells. When it sells, you receive a percentage — typically 50–60% of the sale price. Unsold items are returned to you.

	Wholesale	Consignment
When you get paid	When you deliver the order	When each item sells
Who owns the inventory	The retailer after delivery	You until it sells
Unsold product	Retailer's problem	Comes back to you
Risk	Lower for you — paid upfront	Higher for you — no guaranteed payment
Barrier to entry	Retailer must commit budget	Lower — retailer takes no financial risk
Best for	Proven products with demand	New markets, new stores, testing retail

Consignment is easier to get into because the retailer has nothing to lose financially. They give you shelf space, you provide the product, and you split revenue when it moves. The downside is that you carry all the inventory risk and your cash is tied up until the product sells.

Use consignment strategically. It is an excellent way to get your product into a new city, a new market, or a store with a strong customer base that aligns with your brand — without needing the retailer to make a financial commitment they are not ready for. Think of it as a trial run. If the product moves well on consignment, you have earned the right to have a wholesale conversation.

How to Approach Retailers

The biggest mistake brand owners make when trying to get into stores is showing up without preparation. Walking into a boutique with a sample and asking if they want to carry your brand is not a pitch. It is an interruption. Retailers are busy. They get approached constantly. You need to make it easy for them to say yes.

The Line Sheet

A line sheet is a one or two page document that shows a retailer everything they need to know to place a wholesale order. It is the standard tool for every wholesale conversation in the fashion industry. Without one, you are not ready for the conversation.

- Brand name and logo — clean, professional, immediately recognizable
- Product photography — clear, professional images of every item you are offering for wholesale
- Product names and style numbers — every item needs a reference number
- Available sizes and colorways — everything they can order
- Wholesale price and suggested retail price for each item

- Minimum order quantity (MOQ) — the minimum number of units per style or per order
- Lead time — how long from order placement to delivery
- Your contact information and ordering instructions

Your line sheet should be designed as cleanly as your brand. It is a representation of your brand to a buyer who may not know you yet. If it looks amateur, they will assume the business is amateur. Design it at the same level as everything else you put into the world.

How to Find the Right Retailers

- Start local — boutiques in your city that carry brands in your price range and aesthetic
- Study who already carries similar brands — those buyers understand your customer
- Trade shows — MAGIC in Las Vegas, Agenda, ComplexCon are where buyers actively look for new brands
- Instagram research — find stores that post content aligned with your brand identity
- Direct outreach — a clean, concise email with your line sheet attached, addressed to the buyer by name

The pitch email should be short. Three sentences maximum before you attach the line sheet. Who you are, what you make, why it fits their store. That is it. Make it easy to say yes or easy to ask for more information. Long emails get ignored.

Protecting Yourself in Wholesale and Consignment

Before you put product in any retailer's hands — wholesale or consignment — have a written agreement. For wholesale, confirm the order in writing with payment terms clearly stated. Net-30 (payment 30 days after delivery) is standard but you can negotiate net-15 or even payment upfront for new accounts. For consignment, put a consignment agreement in writing that specifies the split percentage, the reporting schedule, and the timeline for returning unsold inventory.

You do not need a lawyer for basic agreements. Templates are widely available. But get something signed. Handshake deals in retail have cost brand owners thousands of dollars and months of frustration. Protect yourself from the start.

How Wholesale and Consignment Compound Your Brand

The real value of retail partnerships goes beyond the revenue from each order. Every person who discovers your brand in a boutique and then searches for you online becomes a new digital customer. Every store that carries your brand is social proof for the next store you approach. Every wholesale account you land is a line on your brand's credibility story.

Being in the right stores tells potential customers — and future wholesale partners — that your brand has been vetted by someone with buying authority and retail experience. That signal travels. It opens doors that cold outreach alone cannot.

The Lesson

Your website is one channel. Wholesale and consignment are two more. The brands that grow fastest are the ones that build revenue from multiple directions at once — not just the one they started with.

Motivation

Price your product to support wholesale from day one. Build your line sheet before you need it. Get in the right stores. Let the product do the talking.

CHAPTER 45 — Pop-Ups — The Most Underrated Sales Channel in Fashion

I want to talk about something that most brand owners either overlook completely or write off as too much work for too little reward. Pop-ups. Not just as a sales tactic — but as one of the most powerful brand-building tools available to an independent fashion label.

Here is the truth about pop-ups that nobody talks about: the people who show up to a pop-up are not the same people who find you on Instagram. They are a completely different crowd. A different energy. A different kind of buyer. And that difference is exactly why pop-ups are worth doing.

The Crowd You Cannot Reach Any Other Way

Your online audience finds you because an algorithm decided to show them your content, or because they were already looking for something like what you make. Pop-up customers are different. They were not looking for you. They were at an event — a market, a sneaker convention, a streetwear show — and they walked past your table and something stopped them.

That moment of discovery is one of the most powerful things that can happen to a brand. The customer did not scroll to you. They did not click an ad. They walked up to you in the real world, touched the product with their hands, looked at it in person, and made a decision based on the experience. That kind of customer converts at a completely different rate than an online browser. And when they buy, they remember it. They tell people about it. They come back.

The exposure you get at a pop-up — especially events that bring crowds you would never reach on your own — is something no ad budget can fully replicate. It puts your brand in rooms and markets that your digital presence alone will not get you into.

The Events Worth Being At

Not all pop-up events are created equal. The right events bring the right crowd — people who already care about fashion, streetwear, culture, and quality. Here are the categories worth knowing and the specific events worth looking into:

Traveling Streetwear and Sneaker Events

Companies like Sneakercon and Gotsole travel all over the country and produce events in major cities throughout the year. These are not small gatherings. They draw thousands of attendees — sneakerheads, streetwear collectors, and culture-forward consumers who spend money on product they believe in. The crowd is already warmed up before they walk in the door.

What makes these events especially powerful for a growing brand is that you can travel with them. One application, and you can follow the event schedule from city to city — Atlanta, Chicago, Houston, Los Angeles, New York, Miami. Every city is a new market. Every event is a new audience that has never seen your brand before. That kind of national exposure on your own would cost thousands in ads and logistics. As a vendor at a traveling event, you ride the event's marketing, their audience, and their credibility — and you show up with your product.

I have done both Sneakercon and Gotsole. The energy at these events is unlike anything online. The customers engage differently. They ask questions. They compare colorways in person. They try things on. They come back with friends. And when they find a brand they love at an event like this, they follow it long after the event is over.

Streetwear-Specific Markets

The Atlanta Streetwear Market is another event worth being at — and not just because it is local to Atlanta. It is curated. The crowd knows what they are looking for. The vendors are vetted. Being accepted into a curated market like this sends a signal to attendees that your brand belongs in that space. That signal matters.

Curated streetwear markets exist in most major cities. Look for the ones with strong curation, consistent attendance, and an audience that matches your customer profile. A well-run streetwear market will bring more qualified buyers to your table in one afternoon than a poorly targeted ad campaign runs for a week.

Farmers Markets and Community Events

I have not personally done a farmers market, but I want to address it because the opportunity is real and most streetwear brands dismiss it too quickly. Farmers markets and community events bring a local, loyal, foot-traffic crowd. The energy is different from a streetwear event — more casual, more conversational, more community-driven. But that is not a weakness. That is an opportunity.

If your brand has any lifestyle crossover — if it speaks to people beyond just sneakerheads and streetwear collectors — a farmers market or community market puts you in front of a completely different demographic. Professionals, parents, locals who shop small and support independent businesses. These customers become loyal regulars. They come back. They buy as gifts. They are the kind of customer that sustains a brand between the hype drops.

Do not dismiss a venue just because it does not fit the streetwear aesthetic. The question is always: are my customers there? If the answer is yes, you should be there too.

The Independent Pop-Up — Your Own Event in Your Own Market

Beyond attending other people's events, I have also run my own independent pop-ups — booking a space through platforms like Peerspace and creating the entire experience from the ground up in different states. This is a different level of commitment but it delivers a different level of result.

When you run your own pop-up, everything is yours. The environment, the music, the layout, the energy, the customer experience from the moment they walk in to the moment they leave. You are not sharing space with 50 other vendors. You are the destination. The people who show up came specifically for Engineered By Dré. That changes the entire dynamic of the interaction.

Platforms like Peerspace let you book unique spaces — warehouses, studios, rooftops, storefronts — in cities across the country for a fraction of what a traditional retail space would cost. You can test a new market for a weekend, see how the crowd responds, and decide whether it is worth coming back before making any long-term commitment.

Pop-Up Type	Who It Reaches	Best For	Investment Level
Traveling events (Sneakercon, Gotsole)	Sneaker and streetwear consumers nationally	National brand exposure, new city reach	Vendor fee + travel
Curated streetwear markets (ATL Streetwear Market)	Local streetwear community, qualified buyers	Community credibility, local brand building	Vendor fee, usually lower
Farmers markets / community events	Local lifestyle consumers, different demographic	Testing new audiences, community loyalty	Low — most are affordable
Independent pop-up (Peerspace)	Your existing audience + local discovery	Full brand experience, new market testing	Space rental + full setup

How to Make a Pop-Up Work

Showing up is not enough. The brands that win at pop-ups are the ones that treat the table or the space as seriously as they treat their website. The setup communicates the brand before the customer ever touches the product.

- Invest in your display — branded signage, clean folding, consistent visual identity

- Bring your full range — different price points give every customer an entry point
- Capture every customer — have a QR code or sign-up sheet for your email and SMS list
- Have a pop-up exclusive — a product, a colorway, or a discount only available at the event
- Tell people where to find you online before they walk away — card, sticker, or QR code
- Document everything — content from a pop-up performs extremely well because it is real, live, and social

The pop-up exclusive deserves its own emphasis. When you offer something at a pop-up that cannot be purchased online, it creates urgency and exclusivity that drives in-person sales. Customers who are on the fence about a purchase will commit when they understand the opportunity will not exist tomorrow.

The Long-Term Value of Pop-Ups

Every pop-up is not just a sales event. It is a data collection event, a content creation event, a community building event, and a market research event all at the same time. You learn which products people gravitate toward when they can see and touch everything. You hear the questions customers ask repeatedly — those questions are your next FAQ, your next product description, your next piece of content. You meet people who become brand ambassadors, wholesale partners, or collaborators.

The brands that do pop-ups consistently build a physical presence that digital-only brands cannot replicate. Over time, that physical presence compounds. Cities where you have popped up become markets where you have loyal customers. Events where you have appeared become relationships with organizers who keep inviting you back. The crowd you meet in Chicago at a Sneakercon becomes the audience that follows you online when you announce your next drop.

Do not treat pop-ups as a last resort when online sales are slow. Treat them as a pillar of your brand strategy — one of the most human, most direct, and most powerful ways to build the kind of brand loyalty that no algorithm can create.

The Lesson

The customer who discovers you in person and buys face to face is a different kind of customer than the one who clicks an ad. They know you are real. They touched the product. They made a decision in front of you. That customer becomes a brand advocate in a way that online customers rarely do.

Motivation

Get in front of people. Travel with the events. Build your own. Show up to the markets. The room you walk into physically will always open doors that the internet cannot reach.

CHAPTER 46 — How to Get Your Brand in the Hands of Athletes

One of the most powerful moments in Engineered By Dré's early history happened because of a strategy most brand owners would never think to try — and it cost nothing but the product itself and a shipping label.

I sent clothes directly to the practice facility of an NBA team. The practice facility address is public record. I addressed the package to the specific athlete I wanted to gift the product to — Cade Cunningham of the Detroit Pistons — and shipped it in hopes that it would reach him, that he would like it, and that he would wear it. He got it. He liked it. And he wore it in a tunnel shot.

A tunnel shot in the NBA is not a small moment. Players walk into the arena before games dressed intentionally — the tunnel walk has become one of the most watched fashion moments in professional sports. Fans screenshot it. Media covers it. Brands pay hundreds of thousands of dollars to get their product in that shot. I got there by understanding something simple: athletes are people, they receive mail, and their professional facilities have publicly available addresses.

This chapter is about how to use that strategy, how to expand it, and how to think about athlete and celebrity seeding as a brand-building tool — not a paid endorsement play, but a genuine relationship-building strategy.

Why Athletes Matter for a Fashion Brand

Athletes — especially in the NBA, NFL, and other major leagues — have become the most influential figures in streetwear and fashion culture. What they wear to games, to practice, on social media, and in public carries enormous cultural weight. A single photo of an athlete in your product can reach millions of people who already trust that athlete's taste.

The difference between an athlete wearing your brand and an ad showing your brand is credibility. An ad is paid placement — everyone knows it. An athlete choosing to wear something is an endorsement of taste. It signals that the product is good enough, interesting enough, and cool enough to stand on its own without a paid relationship.

That signal is worth more than most marketing budgets can buy. And for an independent brand willing to be creative, it is accessible in ways that most people never discover.

The Practice Facility Strategy — How It Works

Professional sports teams publish or have publicly available addresses for their practice facilities, front offices, and team headquarters. These addresses can be found through:

- The team's official website — many list their facility address in the contact or media section
- Google search — '[Team name] practice facility address' returns results for most major league teams
- Sports databases and media guides — officially published by leagues and teams

- LinkedIn — team staff often list the facility address in their profiles

Once you have the address, you address the package directly to the athlete by name. Include your brand name and a clear return address so it does not look like unsolicited junk mail. The package goes through the team's mailroom, and if the athlete is known at that facility — which they obviously are — it typically reaches them.

Not every package will get through. Not every athlete who receives it will wear it. But the ones who do — and who post it, wear it publicly, or share it with their network — create exposure that no ad campaign can replicate at that cost.

What to Send and How to Package It

The product you send is a representation of your brand. It needs to be your best work — not samples, not seconds, not older inventory you are trying to move. Send the product you are most proud of, packaged at the highest level you can manage.

- Send 1–3 pieces maximum — a curated selection, not a full catalog drop
- Include a handwritten or high-quality printed note — personal, brief, genuine. Tell them who you are, where the brand is from, and why you thought of them specifically
- Package it like a gift, not a shipment — tissue paper, branded packaging, attention to detail
- Include a tag, card, or insert with your brand name, website, and social handle clearly visible
- Do not ask for anything in return — no 'please post this,' no contract, no expectation. Gift it genuinely.

The note matters more than most people think. A generic 'enjoy this gift from our brand' note gets forgotten. A note that references something specific about the athlete — their city, their style, a moment in their career that inspired the design — gets read. And when a note gets read, the product gets considered.

Beyond the Mailroom — Other Ways to Get Product to Athletes

Method	How It Works	Best For
Practice facility mail	Ship directly to team address — addressed to athlete by name	NBA, NFL, MLB, NHL — any major league with public facility addresses
Agent or management outreach	Find the athlete's agency on Google or LinkedIn — email or DM the agent directly	Established athletes with formal representation
Team staff relationship	Build a relationship with a team employee who has internal access	Long-term play — takes time but creates direct pipeline

Method	How It Works	Best For
Events and appearances	Attend events where athletes appear — give the product in person	Most direct — personal interaction creates the strongest impression
Mutual connection	Ask a contact who knows the athlete to pass along the product	When the referral creates context that a cold package cannot
Social media DM	Direct message on Instagram or Twitter with a clear, genuine pitch	Emerging athletes and college players with more accessible inboxes

Which Athletes to Target — Think Strategically

The biggest name is not always the best target. A superstar athlete receives thousands of pieces of product from brands with real budgets and established relationships. Your package is competing with Nike, Jordan Brand, and every major label in the industry.

Think about who is ascending. The second-year player who is about to break out. The rookie with a strong social media presence and a growing fan base. The veteran who is known for having great style but is not yet at a level where every brand is fighting for their attention. These are the athletes where a genuine, quality product can cut through — because the competition for their attention is lower and the relationship potential is higher.

Also think about alignment. The athlete whose lifestyle, city, and aesthetic match what your brand represents will wear it more naturally and more credibly than one who simply has a large following. Cade Cunningham and Engineered By Dré made sense — Detroit connection, his style, the culture around that team at that moment. That alignment is what made the tunnel shot feel genuine rather than forced.

What Happens When It Works — and How to Leverage It

When an athlete wears your product publicly — in a tunnel shot, on social media, at a press conference, or anywhere with visibility — move fast. Screenshot it. Repost it with credit and gratitude. Create content around the moment. Add it to your website. Reference it in your brand story.

That moment is social proof at the highest level. It tells every customer who sees it that your product is good enough for a professional athlete who did not have to wear anything — and chose yours. That credibility has a long shelf life. Use it.

Do not be transactional about the follow-up. Do not immediately DM asking them to post again or sign a deal. Send a genuine thank-you. Build the relationship over time. Some of the most valuable brand partnerships in streetwear started as a gifted package that led to a conversation that led to a collaboration years later. Play the long game.

Expanding the Strategy — Beyond Athletes

The same logic applies beyond professional athletes. Musicians, artists, comedians, content creators, and any public figure with a platform and an alignment with your brand can receive product through similar approaches. Their management contacts are often publicly available. Their tour buses, studios, and production companies have addresses. Their DMs are accessible.

The underlying principle is the same: find the people whose audience overlaps with your customer, send them your best product with genuine intention, and let the product speak for itself. Some will ignore it. Some will wear it once. A few will become genuine advocates. And one moment — one photo, one post, one tunnel walk — can change the trajectory of your brand's visibility permanently.

The Lesson

I sent a package to a practice facility addressed to an NBA player. He wore it in a tunnel shot. That one moment reached more people than months of paid ads. It cost a product and a shipping label. It worked because the product was great, the packaging was intentional, and the strategy was creative.

Motivation

Find the people whose platform can amplify your brand. Get your product in their hands. Let the quality do the convincing. The creative strategy that nobody else is doing is often the one that works the best.

CHAPTER 47 — The Details That Make Your Brand Unforgettable

There is a moment every customer has when they receive an order. They pick up the package. They open it. And in those first few seconds, before they ever see the product itself, they have already formed an impression about the brand that sent it.

Most brands fail that moment. The product arrives in a plain poly bag, folded loosely, with nothing else inside. It feels like a transaction. It feels like Amazon. It does not feel like a brand that invested in what they created.

The brands that build lasting loyalty — the ones customers talk about, post about, and come back to — are the ones that treat the unboxing experience as part of the product itself. Every touchpoint from the moment the package arrives to the moment the customer puts the garment on is an opportunity to reinforce who you are and why they made the right decision buying from you.

This is not about being expensive. It is about being intentional. Most of what separates a memorable brand experience from a forgettable one costs very little. It just requires thought.

The Unboxing Is Part of the Product

Think about the last time you received something that genuinely impressed you before you even touched the product. What was it? Probably the packaging. The way it was folded. Something unexpected inside. A note that felt personal. A detail that signaled care.

That feeling is what your customers can have every single time they open a package from you — if you design for it. And when customers feel that way, they share it. Unboxing content is one of the most organic, authentic forms of social proof a fashion brand can generate. A customer who films their unboxing because the experience was worth filming is doing your marketing for you without being asked.

The Elements That Elevate the Experience

Packaging — The First Impression Before the Product

Your outer packaging — the poly bag, box, or mailer — is the first physical thing the customer touches. It communicates quality before anything is opened. A branded poly bag with your logo printed on it costs very little more than a plain one. A custom box elevates the perception of everything inside it. A kraft paper mailer with a custom stamp or sticker signals handcrafted care.

- Branded poly bags — your logo printed on the bag instead of a plain clear or black bag
- Custom mailer boxes — especially for higher-ticket items, a box that looks intentional changes the entire experience
- Tissue paper — folding the garment in branded or colored tissue paper adds a luxury feel at minimal cost
- Custom tape — branded tape sealing the package is a small detail that registers immediately
- Stickers on the outside — a brand sticker sealing the tissue paper or placed on the package adds personality before it is even opened

What Goes Inside — The Details That Get Remembered

What is inside the package alongside the product tells the customer who you are as a brand. These are the touchpoints that get photographed, talked about, and remembered.

Insert	What It Communicates	Cost Level
Hang tags	Premium product identity — a well-designed hang tag makes even a simple garment feel intentional	Low — $0.10–$0.50 per tag at volume
Branded stickers	Community and culture — customers put stickers on laptops, water bottles, cars. Your brand travels.	Very low — $0.05–$0.20 each at volume

Insert	What It Communicates	Cost Level
Thank you card	Personal connection — a simple card signed or personalized makes the customer feel seen, not processed	Very low — printed cards under $0.25 each
Brand lookbook or mini catalog	Aspiration — shows customers the full world your brand represents, creates desire for the next purchase	Low to moderate
Care instructions card	Professionalism — tells the customer you care about the product lasting, builds trust in quality	Very low
QR code card	Digital bridge — links to your social, your next drop, your review page, or a video from you	Free to create, tiny to print
Free gift	Delight — something unexpected that costs almost nothing but creates a memorable moment	Varies — stickers, pins, keychains

Hang Tags — The Most Underused Branding Tool in Fashion

A hang tag is attached to the garment and is one of the first things a customer sees when they pull the product out. Most brands either skip them entirely or use generic white tags with a printed logo. The brands that understand branding treat the hang tag as a creative asset.

Your hang tag can include your brand name and logo, the garment name or style number, care instructions, a QR code linking to your story or social media, a short brand statement or quote, and the garment's place of origin. All of that on a card the size of a business card, attached with a cotton cord or branded string, tells the customer they purchased from a brand that cares about every detail.

The difference in cost between a generic hang tag and a well-designed one is small. The difference in perceived value is not.

Stickers — The Free Marketing You Are Not Using

A sticker in every package is one of the highest ROI brand investments you can make. Here is why: a customer who puts your sticker on their laptop, water bottle, car, or notebook is carrying your brand into every environment they enter. Other people see it. They ask about it. It starts conversations your ads could never start.

Stickers travel. They get photographed. They end up in places you never planned for. A brand with a great sticker design has a piece of marketing collateral that customers actively want — and will display voluntarily. That is the definition of earned media.

Include at least one sticker in every order. Make the design worth displaying. Your best sticker is the one that works as a standalone design — something someone would put on their personal belongings because they think it looks cool, not just because it has your name on it.

The Thank You Note — The Detail That Creates Loyalty

A handwritten thank you note is not scalable forever. But in the early stages of building your brand, writing a short personal note in every package creates a level of connection that no automated email can replicate. Customers who receive a handwritten note feel like a person sent their order, not a warehouse. They remember it. They talk about it.

As the brand grows and handwriting every note becomes impractical, a high-quality printed card with a genuine message in your voice accomplishes much of the same effect. The key is that it feels personal — not corporate. Signed with your name. Written in your voice. Brief and genuine.

Something as simple as: 'Thank you for supporting what we're building. Every order means something to us. — André' costs almost nothing to produce and creates a feeling that most brands in this industry do not bother to create.

Pop-Up Packaging — The In-Person Version

The same philosophy applies at pop-ups. The bag you put a customer's purchase in at an event is the last thing they carry away. A branded bag with your logo — even a simple kraft paper bag with a sticker — communicates that you thought about their experience beyond the transaction. It travels through the event. Other attendees see it. It becomes a walking advertisement that the customer paid for.

- Use branded bags at every pop-up — even a simple paper bag with your sticker is better than a plain plastic bag
- Wrap the product in tissue paper even at in-person events — it adds to the perceived value
- Include a sticker or business card with every in-person purchase — give them something to take home beyond the product
- Consider a QR code card pointing to your online store — in-person customers who love the product need an easy path back

The Investment Perspective — What This Actually Costs

Item	Approximate Cost at Volume	What It Returns
Branded poly bags (500 units)	$60–$120	Premium first impression on every order

Item	Approximate Cost at Volume	What It Returns
Hang tags (500 units)	$50–$100	Elevated perceived product value
Stickers (500 units)	$30–$75	Organic brand placement in customers' lives
Thank you cards (500 units)	$40–$80	Customer loyalty and word of mouth
Tissue paper (500 sheets)	$20–$40	Luxury unboxing feel
Total investment per 500 orders	~$200–$415	~$0.40–$0.83 per order

Less than one dollar per order to make every customer feel like they bought from a premium brand. That is one of the highest-return investments available to you. A brand that charges $150 for a workshirt and ships it in a plain poly bag with nothing inside is creating a disconnect between the price and the experience. A brand that charges $150 and ships it in branded tissue paper with a hang tag, a sticker, and a thank you card is reinforcing that the price was worth it — before the customer even puts the shirt on.

Where to Source These Materials

- Sticker Mule — high quality stickers, hang tags, and packaging at competitive prices with small minimums
- Alibaba — custom poly bags, tissue paper, boxes, and packaging at scale for larger orders
- Canva or Adobe Illustrator — design your hang tags, stickers, and cards yourself before sending to print
- Vistaprint or Moo — thank you cards and business cards at low minimums
- Packlane or noissue — premium custom boxes and tissue paper with eco-friendly options
- Your local print shop — for small runs or quick turnarounds, a local printer can be faster and more flexible

---

The Lesson

The product is what they bought. The experience is what they remember. A great product in forgettable packaging is a missed opportunity. A great product in intentional packaging is a brand.

Motivation

Invest in the details. A sticker, a hang tag, a note — these are not extras. They are the difference between a customer who bought once and a customer who comes back, tells their friends, and posts their unboxing. Engineer the experience from the first touch to the last.

CHAPTER 48 — Collaborations — When to Do Them, When to Walk Away, and How to Structure Them

My first collaboration with the Detroit Pistons — I paid for the bulk order myself. I covered the manufacturing cost, the production, everything. What I received in return was the right to use their marketing, their channels, their credibility, and their audience to amplify Engineered By Dré.

Most people would look at that and say I got the short end of the deal. I disagree. That collaboration built a relationship. It proved what I could deliver. It showed the Pistons organization that Engineered By Dré could execute at a professional level and produce something their fanbase responded to.

The second time we collaborated — they paid for the bulk order and paid me a design fee on top of it.

That is the arc of a collaboration done correctly. The first one was an investment. The second one was a return. Understanding that arc — and knowing how to navigate it — is what separates brand owners who build lasting partnership equity from ones who either miss opportunities or get taken advantage of.

What a Collaboration Actually Is

A collaboration is a creative and commercial partnership between two brands, organizations, or individuals who bring different value to the same project. The value each party brings determines the structure of the deal — who pays, who gets paid, what each side receives, and what the long-term relationship looks like.

Collaborations come in many forms in fashion:

Collaboration Type	Example	What Each Party Brings
Independent brand x Major organization	EBD x Detroit Pistons	Brand brings design and product. Organization brings audience, credibility, and distribution.
Independent brand x Independent brand	Two streetwear brands co-releasing a product	Both bring their audiences, aesthetics, and production capabilities
Brand x Artist or Designer	Brand produces, artist creates the visual concept	Brand brings manufacturing. Artist brings creative and their audience.
Brand x Influencer or Athlete	Product gifted or co-designed with a public figure	Brand brings product. Influencer/athlete brings reach and credibility.

Collaboration Type	Example	What Each Party Brings
Brand x Corporate / National Company	EBD x Wingstop	Brand brings culture and authenticity. Corporation brings scale and budget.

When a Collaboration Adds Value

Not every collaboration is worth doing. The ones that add value share certain characteristics — and recognizing them before you commit is what protects both your brand and your time.

- Audience alignment — the other party's audience overlaps meaningfully with your customer. Their fanbase should be people who would genuinely buy your product.
- Creative alignment — the collaboration makes sense visually and culturally. It should feel natural, not forced. When a collaboration looks like it belongs, it converts. When it looks like a sponsorship, it does not.
- Mutual legitimacy lift — both parties come out of the collaboration more credible than they went in. The best collaborations elevate both brands.
- Clear production path — you know how the product gets made, who pays for what, and what the timeline looks like before you agree to anything.
- Long-term relationship potential — the collaboration is a door, not just a transaction. The best partnerships lead to the next one.

When a Collaboration Depreciates Your Brand

Not every opportunity with a big name is actually a good opportunity. Some collaborations damage the brand more than they help it — and the damage is not always obvious until it has already happened.

Red Flag	What It Signals
The partner's values contradict your brand identity	Customers will notice the disconnect — it undermines your credibility
You are being used as a diversity checkbox	The relationship is transactional, not genuine — it shows
The terms require you to compromise your design standards	A collaboration that produces inferior product hurts both your brand and the partner's
The financial terms are exploitative	Being paid nothing while generating significant value for a large organization sets a bad precedent
The partner has controversial public perception	Their reputation attaches to yours whether you want it to or not

Red Flag	What It Signals
It is a one-time transaction with no relationship building	If there is no path to a second collaboration, evaluate whether the first is worth it

The most important question to ask before any collaboration is: does this make my brand stronger or does it make my brand confusing? If the answer is anything other than stronger — walk away. A missed opportunity you chose to pass on is always better than a collaboration you regret.

How to Structure the Deal — The Financial Framework

Collaboration structures vary widely depending on who you are working with, what you bring to the table, and what stage your brand is at. Here are the most common structures and when each makes sense:

Structure 1 — You Pay, You Own the Exposure

You fund the production entirely and the partner provides marketing, audience access, and credibility. This is what my first Detroit Pistons collaboration looked like. You take on the financial risk but you receive something that money cannot always buy directly: association with a major brand and access to their audience.

When this makes sense: when the exposure opportunity is genuinely transformative for your brand and you can afford the production cost without putting the business at risk. When the relationship has long-term potential that justifies the upfront investment. When you are in the early stages and need the credibility lift more than you need the margin.

When this does not make sense: when the production cost would strain the business. When the partner's audience is not actually your customer. When there is no path to a more equitable second collaboration.

Structure 2 — They Pay, You Design

The partner funds the production and pays you a design fee for your creative work. This is what the second Detroit Pistons collaboration looked like. This is the structure you work toward — it means the relationship has matured and the partner now understands the value you bring.

This structure is standard in established brand partnerships. The larger organization has the budget and the brand provides the creative direction, the cultural authenticity, and the product execution. The design fee compensates you for your time, expertise, and brand equity being attached to the product.

What is a fair design fee? It depends on the scale of the collaboration, the partner's budget, and your brand's leverage. Start by calculating what your time and expertise are worth. Early collaborations with major organizations might start at $2,000–$5,000 for a design fee. As your brand grows and the relationship deepens, that number should reflect the value you bring — not just the hours you put in.

Structure 3 — Revenue Split

Both parties contribute — one brings production, one brings distribution or marketing — and revenue is split based on an agreed percentage. This is common in brand x brand collaborations where both parties are investing and both parties are selling.

The split should reflect the actual contribution of each party. If you are providing the product and they are providing the store and the audience, a 50/50 split is not automatically fair — the contribution of the larger audience may warrant a different ratio. Negotiate based on value, not just effort.

Always get the revenue split in writing before production begins. Include how revenue is tracked, when payouts happen, and what happens to unsold inventory. These details create problems when they are assumed and not documented.

Structure 4 — Working for Free — When It Is Strategic

There are times when the right financial structure is no payment at all. This is not desperation — it is strategy. When the exposure, the relationship, or the credential is worth more than any fee you could charge, working for free or at cost is a legitimate business decision.

The Detroit Pistons first collaboration was essentially working at cost. I did not make margin on that production — I covered my costs and invested the rest in the relationship. That investment returned a paid design fee and covered production on the second collaboration. The return on the first 'free' collaboration was significant.

Working for free makes sense when:

- The partner's audience is genuinely transformative for your brand's visibility
- The relationship has clear long-term upside that a one-time fee cannot capture
- The collaboration credential strengthens your position for future paid deals — being able to say 'we collaborated with [major organization]' opens doors
- The production cost is manageable and does not strain the business
- You have a clear understanding of what you want to get out of it beyond money

Working for free does not make sense when:

- The production cost would damage the business
- The partner has the budget to pay and is simply leveraging your eagerness
- There is no genuine path to a paid relationship — you are just being used
- The exposure does not actually reach your customer — a big name with the wrong audience is not worth the investment

Protecting Yourself in Every Collaboration

Regardless of the structure — whether you are paying, they are paying, or the work is free — certain protections must be in place before any product is made or any design is delivered.

- Written agreement — every collaboration needs a contract. Who owns the design IP, who owns the product inventory, how revenue is split, what each party is permitted to do with the collaboration's imagery and assets.
- Design ownership — by default, when you create a design for a collaboration, you own that design unless the contract specifies otherwise. Do not assume they own it. Do not assume you can reuse it. Define it in writing.
- Exclusivity — does this collaboration prevent you from working with a competitor? For how long? This should be explicitly defined and compensated if it limits your business.
- Approval rights — you should have approval over how your brand name and logo are used in any collaboration's marketing materials. Your brand's presentation is your responsibility.
- Timeline and delivery — define when the product is needed, who handles fulfillment, and what happens if either party fails to deliver on schedule.

Small Brand Collaborations — Why They Matter Too

The focus on major organizations like the Pistons and Wingstop is instructive — but do not overlook collaborations with other independent brands. A well-executed collaboration between two independent brands with aligned audiences can generate significant mutual benefit at a fraction of the complexity of a corporate partnership.

Two brands each bringing 10,000 highly engaged followers to a shared product creates a combined audience of 20,000 people who are already warm. Both brands get introduced to a new audience that trusts the brand that vouched for them. The product becomes a bridge between two communities — and both communities grow stronger for it.

Small brand collaborations also build the portfolio that earns you the bigger ones. The path to a corporate partnership often runs through a track record of successful independent collaborations that demonstrate you can execute, you can market, and you can build something worth being associated with.

The Collaboration Mindset — Long Game Thinking

Every collaboration is a chapter in a relationship that has the potential to extend far beyond the product itself. The brands that build the most powerful collaboration portfolios are the ones that approach every partnership with the question: how do I make this so good that they come back?

When you over-deliver on a collaboration — when the product exceeds what was expected, the marketing is stronger than they planned for, and the execution is flawless — you do not just complete a deal. You create a partner who advocates for you in rooms you are not in yet. Who recommends you to other organizations. Who comes back with a bigger budget and more creative freedom.

That is what happened with the Detroit Pistons. The first collaboration was investment. The second was return. The third and beyond is compound interest.

The Lesson

The first collaboration is rarely about the money. It is about proving what you are capable of, building the relationship, and earning the right to a better deal next time. Play the first one like an investment. Execute it like a portfolio piece. Let the quality negotiate the next deal for you.

Motivation

Know when to work for free. Know when to charge. Know when to walk away. The collaboration that builds your brand's future is worth more than the one that pays you once and goes nowhere.

CHAPTER 49 — Operations — Home, Warehouse, Virtual Address & Business Phone

Where you operate from, how you present that location to the world, and how people reach you are not just logistical decisions. They are financial decisions, security decisions, and credibility decisions that affect everything from your ability to get a business loan to whether a manufacturer takes you seriously on a first call.

Most brand owners treat these as afterthoughts. They operate from their home, use their personal address on everything, and answer customer calls on their personal cell phone. That approach limits your access to capital, exposes your personal information to the public, and signals to professional partners that the business is not yet running like a business.

This chapter covers how to think about your physical operations at every stage — home, warehouse, and everything in between — and two tools that every brand owner should have from day one regardless of where they operate: a virtual address and a dedicated business phone number.

Stage 1 — Operating From Home

Most brands start here. It is the right move. Overhead is low, the commute is zero, and the money that would go to rent goes to inventory and growth instead. There is no shame in a home operation — some of the most successful brands in streetwear started in a bedroom or a garage. I started in my home, moved to my garage, then to a commercial space.

The home operation works well when:

- Order volume is manageable — you can pack and ship without overwhelming your living space
- Inventory can be stored without taking over the entire home

- You are the primary fulfillment person — no team yet or a very small one
- Cash is better deployed into product and marketing than into commercial rent

The home operation starts to break down when inventory storage consumes too much space, when order volume creates a daily packing operation that takes hours, when you need team members working alongside you regularly, or when the separation between personal life and business life disappears entirely. Those are the signals that a workspace transition is coming.

Stage 2 — Moving Into a Warehouse or Commercial Space

The decision to move into a commercial space should be driven by necessity and financial readiness — not by the desire to look more established. Premature warehouse overhead has killed brands that were otherwise healthy. Wait until the home operation is genuinely at capacity before making the move.

Sign It Is Time to Move	What It Means
Inventory consumes entire rooms in your home	Storage space is the operational ceiling
Packing and shipping takes 4+ hours daily	Fulfillment is consuming time meant for building
You need team members working on-site consistently	Home space does not support a team operation
Commercial partners or wholesale buyers want to visit	A home address is not appropriate for professional meetings
Revenue consistently supports the added overhead	The rent does not strain the business — it enables it
The business has outgrown the lifestyle of a home operation	Mental and operational separation from work becomes necessary

When you do move into a commercial space, protect the location. Your warehouse address is not public information. It is not on your website, not in your email signature, not on your social media. The public address for your brand is your virtual address — not your warehouse. This is not paranoia. It is security. A public warehouse location creates risk — theft, unwanted visits, safety concerns for your team. Keep it private.

I have never publicly disclosed my warehouse location. Every communication, every business registration, every public-facing document uses my virtual address. The warehouse exists to fulfill orders — not to receive the public.

The Virtual Address — Why Every Brand Owner Needs One From Day One

A virtual address is a real street address — not a P.O. box — at a commercial location that you rent the use of. Services like iPostal1, Regus, Alliance Virtual Offices, and similar providers give you a legitimate business address at a real building in a real city.

Your mail is received there, scanned and forwarded to you digitally, and you can access it without ever going to the location.

This is not a loophole or a gray area. It is a standard business service used by millions of legitimate companies. And it solves several serious problems simultaneously.

Problem Without Virtual Address	How Virtual Address Solves It
Home address on all business documents — privacy risk	Business address is the virtual location — home stays private
Warehouse address public — security risk	Virtual address is the public face — warehouse stays private
Home address on LLC registration — searchable public record	Virtual address on LLC — personal address not in public filings
Banks deny business loans — 'no business address'	Virtual address qualifies as a legitimate business address for banking
Manufacturers and partners see a residential address	Commercial address signals an established operation
Difficult to open certain business accounts without an address	Virtual address satisfies the business address requirement

The Banking and Loan Access Reality

Here is something most brand owners discover the hard way: when you apply for a business loan, a business line of credit, or certain business bank accounts, the bank looks at your business address. A home address raises flags. It signals to underwriters that the business may not be operating at a commercial scale — even if your revenue tells a completely different story.

A virtual address at a commercial location — especially one in a recognizable business district or office building — changes that perception. It tells the bank that the business has a legitimate commercial presence. In some cases, it is the difference between an approval and a denial on a loan application that your revenue would otherwise support.

Some virtual address providers are specifically set up to support business banking and SBA loan applications. When choosing a virtual address service, confirm that the address is acceptable for business registration in your state and for business banking purposes. Not all virtual addresses are equal — a legitimate commercial building address is more powerful than a mailbox store address.

I use a virtual address for all of my business registrations, banking, and public-facing communications. It is one of the lowest-cost, highest-impact infrastructure decisions I made for the brand.

Where to Get a Virtual Address

- iPostal1 — one of the most widely accepted for business banking and LLC registration, real street addresses, mail scanning included
- Regus / IWG — global network of real office buildings, prestigious addresses, higher cost but maximum credibility
- Alliance Virtual Offices — affordable, real street addresses, mail forwarding and scanning
- Davinci Virtual — real addresses, live receptionist options, good for professional service businesses
- Your local coworking space — many offer a mail address service for a small monthly fee — local and legitimate

Cost ranges from $10 to $50 per month depending on the provider and address location. It is one of the least expensive and most impactful investments in your business infrastructure.

The Business Phone Number — Why Your Personal Number Should Never Be Your Business Number

Your personal cell phone number is not your business phone number. It should never be listed on your website, your business cards, your LLC registration, your bank accounts, or any public-facing business document. Using your personal number for business creates problems that are easy to avoid and difficult to undo.

Problem With Personal Number for Business	Why It Matters
Your personal number becomes publicly associated with the brand	You lose the ability to separate personal and business communication permanently
Customers, vendors, and spam callers have your personal contact	Your personal phone never stops ringing for business reasons
Banks and financial institutions record your personal number as business contact	Mixing personal and business financial identity weakens your business credit structure
If you ever sell the business, your personal number is embedded everywhere	Extraction is painful and sometimes impossible
Personal number on LLC creates a public record link to you personally	Privacy and security implications, especially as the brand grows

The solution is simple and inexpensive: get a dedicated business phone number from day one. You do not need a second physical phone. You need a second number that rings on your existing phone or through an app.

How to Get a Business Phone Number

- Google Voice — free business number that rings on your existing phone. Works for most early-stage brand needs. Limitations on business banking use.
- OpenPhone — purpose-built business phone system, excellent for small teams, shared numbers, call routing, voicemail transcription. Starts at $15/month.
- Grasshopper — virtual phone system designed for small businesses. Professional auto-attendant, extensions, call forwarding. Starts at $28/month.
- RingCentral — more robust for growing teams with multiple lines and departments.
- Your carrier — many carriers offer a second line on your existing plan for $10–$15/month. Simple but less feature-rich.

For most early-stage brand owners, Google Voice or OpenPhone covers everything needed. The number appears on all business documents, answers calls professionally, and keeps your personal number completely separate.

What to Use Your Business Number For

- Your Shopify store contact number — customers contact the business, not you personally
- Business bank accounts and credit applications — all financial institutions use the business number
- LLC and business registration documents — public records show the business number
- Manufacturer and vendor communication — professional relationships use the business line
- Virtual address and mail services — contact number on file with address provider
- Business cards and marketing materials — the number that represents the brand

Your personal number stays personal. It is for friends, family, and relationships that exist outside the brand. The moment your personal number becomes your business number, you lose the ability to ever separate the two.

The Business Email — Your Brand's Professional Voice

Your email address communicates credibility before the person receiving it reads a single word. An email from shop@engineeredbydre.com tells the recipient they are dealing with a real business. An email from engineeredbydre2023@gmail.com tells them they are dealing with someone who has not set up their business properly yet.

This is not a small detail. Manufacturers, wholesale buyers, collaboration partners, media contacts, and financial institutions all form an impression based on your email address. A professional branded email — one that uses your domain — signals that you have invested in the brand's infrastructure. A free personal email signals the opposite.

Personal / Free Email	Branded Business Email
ebdre@gmail.com	shop@engineeredbydre.com

Personal / Free Email	Branded Business Email
Signals: individual, not established	Signals: professional brand, real business
No domain ownership implied	Domain ownership confirmed
Rejected or flagged by some financial institutions	Accepted by all professional and financial contacts
Difficult to hand off if you hire team members	Can create multiple addresses (support@, orders@, collab@)
Mixed with personal communication	Fully separated — business stays business

How to Set Up a Business Email

You need two things: a domain name and an email hosting service.

- Domain — purchase your brand's domain through GoDaddy, Namecheap, or Shopify Domains. yourbrand.com is the foundation. If you already have a Shopify store, your domain is likely already purchased.
- Google Workspace — $6 per user per month. Gives you a fully branded Gmail address (yourname@yourbrand.com), Google Drive, Google Calendar, and the full Google productivity suite under your brand's domain. This is the standard for small businesses and the most widely accepted email platform for professional communication.
- Microsoft 365 — similar to Google Workspace, preferred by some corporate partners. Starts at $6/month. Includes Outlook, Word, Excel, and Teams.

For most brand owners, Google Workspace is the right choice. It integrates with Shopify, Klaviyo, and almost every other tool in your stack. It is familiar, reliable, and universally accepted.

Email Addresses to Set Up

- shop@yourbrand.com or hello@yourbrand.com — your primary contact address, listed on your website and all business documents
- support@yourbrand.com — customer service address, can be forwarded to the same inbox or managed by a team member
- collab@yourbrand.com — for collaboration and partnership inquiries — separates business development from operational email
- orders@yourbrand.com — optional but useful for order-specific communication

You do not need to manage multiple inboxes. All of these addresses can forward to one inbox and you respond from the appropriate address. The point is that the person contacting you sees a professional, organized business — not a single person managing everything from one Gmail account.

Your email address is your digital handshake. Make it represent the brand the same way your packaging and your product do.

The Full Infrastructure Picture

When you put these pieces together — virtual address, business phone number, business email, LLC, business bank account, business credit profile — you have built a complete, professional business infrastructure that is entirely separate from your personal identity. This separation protects you legally, financially, and practically.

Infrastructure Layer	Tool	Monthly Cost
Business address	Virtual address (iPostal1, Alliance, Regus)	$10–$50/month
Business phone	OpenPhone, Grasshopper, or Google Voice	$0–$28/month
Business banking	Relay, Mercury, or local bank business account	Free or low fee
Business email	Google Workspace (yourname@yourbrand.com)	$6/month
Business bookkeeping	Wave (free) or QuickBooks	$0–$30/month
LLC registration	State filing fee	One-time $50–$500

Total monthly cost of a complete professional business infrastructure: approximately $26–$114 per month. For a brand doing any meaningful revenue, this is one of the most efficient investments you can make. Everything about your brand communicates to the world that it is real, serious, and built to last.

The Lesson

Where you operate from is temporary. How you present your business to the world is permanent — until you deliberately change it. A virtual address, a business phone number, and a branded email address cost less than $60 a month combined. They unlock banking access, protect your privacy, and signal to every partner, manufacturer, and financial institution that you are operating a real business.

Motivation

Get the virtual address. Get the business number. Get the business email. Keep your warehouse private. Keep your personal life separate. Build the infrastructure that protects the brand and the person building it.

CHAPTER 50 — Shipping Strategy — How to Get Orders There and Keep Customers Happy

Shipping is the last mile of the customer experience. Everything you did right — the product, the packaging, the purchase — can be undone by a shipping experience that is slow, expensive, or unreliable. And yet most brand owners treat shipping as an afterthought instead of a strategy.

Your shipping strategy directly affects conversion rate, average order value, customer satisfaction, and your cost structure. Every decision — which carriers you use, how you price shipping, how you communicate tracking, how you handle problems — compounds into either a competitive advantage or a persistent source of customer complaints.

How to Price Shipping

Shipping Model	How It Works	Best For	Watch Out For
Free shipping	You absorb the cost into your margins or product price	High-ticket items where margin supports it — increases conversion rate	Can destroy margin on low-ticket items or heavy products
Flat rate shipping	One fixed price regardless of order size — e.g. $7.99 per order	Consistent product weights — simple and predictable for customers	Heavy or oversized orders lose money; very small orders may overprice
Calculated shipping	Real-time carrier rates at checkout based on weight and destination	Wide product range with different weights and sizes	Can surprise customers with high rates — add handling buffer
Free over threshold	Free shipping on orders over $X — e.g. free over $100	Increases average order value — customers add items to hit the threshold	Set the threshold at a level that actually protects your margin

The free shipping threshold is one of the most effective AOV tools available. When a customer is at $85 and free shipping kicks in at $100, they will often add a $20 accessory rather than pay $8 in shipping. The math works for both parties — they get free shipping, you get a larger order. Set the threshold at a level that covers your average shipping cost while encouraging the add-on.

Which Carriers to Use and When

Carrier	Best For	Notes
USPS First Class	Lightweight packages under 1 lb — accessories, small items	Cheapest for light items — no weekend surcharge
USPS Priority Mail	Packages 1–5 lbs — most garments	2–3 day delivery, includes some insurance, flat rate boxes available
UPS Ground	Heavier packages — bulk items, multiple garments in one order	Competitive for packages over 2 lbs going short distances
FedEx Ground / Home	Heavier packages, residential delivery	Competitive rates, good tracking, strong for e-commerce
DHL Express	International orders	Fastest and most reliable for international — worth the premium
Shopify Shipping	All carriers — discounted rates negotiated by Shopify	Always compare Shopify rates first — often cheaper than going direct

Use Shopify Shipping for all domestic orders — the pre-negotiated rates are almost always lower than what you can get going directly to USPS, UPS, or FedEx. For international, compare DHL Express rates through Shopify against going directly. For very high-volume brands, contact carriers directly to negotiate custom rates based on volume.

Communicating Shipping to Customers

- State your processing time clearly on every product page and in your cart — '3–5 business days processing + shipping time'
- Send automated tracking emails the moment a label is created — Shopify does this by default, make sure it is turned on
- Set realistic expectations rather than aspirational ones — under-promise and over-deliver
- For custom or preorder products, clearly state the production timeline before purchase — not in fine print, prominently

When Packages Get Lost or Damaged

It will happen. A package will get lost in the USPS system. A carrier will damage a shipment. A customer will claim they never received something that tracking shows as delivered. How you handle these moments defines whether you keep the customer or lose them forever.

- Always purchase shipping insurance on orders over $100 — the cost is minimal relative to the claim value
- File carrier claims promptly — most carriers have time limits on claims (usually 60–90 days from ship date)
- Reship quickly for confirmed lost or damaged packages — do not make the customer wait weeks for a resolution
- For 'delivered but not received' claims — check with neighbors, verify the delivery photo, then use your judgment. Most customers are honest. The ones who are not will show patterns over time.
- Document everything — keep shipping receipts and tracking numbers for every order for at least 90 days

---

The Lesson

Shipping is not the last step in the process. It is the last impression. A fast, clearly communicated, problem-free shipping experience turns first-time buyers into repeat customers. A slow, confusing, unresolved shipping problem turns them into bad reviews.

Motivation

Engineer your shipping strategy the same way you engineer your product. Know your costs, communicate clearly, and resolve problems faster than the customer expects.

CHAPTER 51 — Returns and Exchanges — How to Turn a Problem Into Loyalty

Returns and exchanges are not signs that your brand is failing. They are a normal part of running a fashion business. What matters is not whether they happen — they will — but how you handle them when they do.

Most brand owners dread returns. The best ones treat every return as information. A return tells you something about your product, your sizing, your descriptions, or your customer's expectations. When you read that information correctly and respond to it systematically, returns become one of the most useful data sources in the business.

Setting Up a Return and Exchange Policy That Works

Your return policy should do three things: protect the business from abuse, give genuine customers a fair resolution, and be clear enough that it reduces support tickets by answering questions before they are asked.

- Define the window clearly — 30 days from delivery is standard for most fashion brands
- Define what is eligible — unworn, unwashed, with original tags attached
- Define what is not eligible — custom or personalized items, final sale items, worn or washed items

- Define the process — how does the customer initiate a return? Email? An online portal? Who pays for return shipping?
- Define the resolution options — refund to original payment, store credit, or exchange

Store credit as the default resolution option is worth considering. It keeps the revenue in the business while still solving the customer's problem. Pair it with a slightly higher credit amount than the original purchase price — 'we'll give you $X in store credit, which is $10 more than the refund value' — and most customers will take the credit, which leads to another purchase.

Using Return Data to Improve the Business

Return Reason	What It Tells You	What to Fix
Wrong size ordered	Size chart is unclear or inaccurate	Update size chart, add fit notes to product description
Product looked different in photos	Photography does not accurately represent the product	Improve product photography — add more angles and real-life context
Quality not as expected	Product description oversells the quality	Either improve the product or be more accurate in the description
Changed mind	No actionable product issue — customer preference	Review your return policy window and final sale designations
Defective product	Manufacturing quality control issue	Report to manufacturer, review sampling process
Arrived too late	Shipping expectation not met	Update shipping timeline communication on product pages

Track your return reasons every month. When one reason appears repeatedly, it is not bad luck. It is a signal. Fix the signal source and the return rate drops. A healthy return rate for a fashion brand is 5–15%. Above 20% consistently means something structural is wrong with the product, the photography, or the description.

Turning a Return Into a Retained Customer

The way you handle a return determines whether you keep the relationship. A customer who had a friction-free return experience and received a fair, fast resolution is more likely to purchase again than a customer who never had any issue at all — because you proved you stand behind what you sell.

- Respond to return requests within 24 hours — speed signals that you care

- Be generous in the resolution — a $10 store credit on top of the return cost almost nothing and creates loyalty
- Follow up after the return is processed — 'how was your experience?' shows you value the relationship beyond the transaction
- If the return was due to a defect — apologize genuinely and replace the item without requiring the return of the defective piece

---

The Lesson

Returns are not the enemy. Mishandled returns are. Every return is a chance to prove that your brand stands behind what it sells. The customer who returns something and walks away thinking 'that was handled beautifully' will be back.

Motivation

Track the reasons. Fix the sources. Handle every return with the speed and generosity that you would want if you were the customer.

CHAPTER 52 — Overselling, Inventory Management & Reducing Human Error

Overselling is one of the most damaging operational problems an e-commerce brand can have. A customer purchases a product, receives an order confirmation, and then gets an email days later telling them the item they bought is actually out of stock. That experience destroys trust in a way that is very difficult to recover from. The customer feels misled. They feel like the brand is not organized enough to know what it has. And often, they do not come back.

I ran into overselling problems early in building Engineered By Dré. When demand is high and orders are coming in fast, inventory levels can move faster than the systems tracking them. What I learned — sometimes the hard way — is that overselling is almost always a systems problem, not a people problem. And systems problems have systems solutions.

How Overselling Happens

- Inventory counts are not updated in real time across all selling channels
- Multiple people have access to fulfill orders and there is no single source of truth for inventory levels
- Products are listed on multiple platforms (Shopify, pop-up POS, wholesale) and inventory is not synced
- Buffer stock is not built into the available inventory count — what is listed as available is also what is physically needed for safety stock
- Manual inventory counts introduce human error — miscounts, transposition errors, items marked as in stock that were damaged
- Pre-orders and regular orders are not separated in the inventory system — causing confusion about what is available to ship immediately

How to Set Up Inventory Management That Prevents Overselling

The solution starts with Shopify's built-in inventory tracking — but it requires intentional configuration and discipline to maintain.

- Turn on 'Track quantity' for every product variant in Shopify — without this, Shopify has no way to prevent overselling
- Set 'Continue selling when out of stock' to OFF for items you cannot immediately restock — this prevents purchases beyond your available inventory
- Build a buffer into your listed inventory — if you have 50 units, list 45 as available. The 5-unit buffer protects you from the gap between a sale and the inventory update processing
- Conduct physical inventory counts weekly — especially before drops and during high-volume periods
- Use a single fulfillment location in Shopify — avoid splitting inventory across multiple locations unless your systems can handle the sync
- Separate pre-order inventory from ready-to-ship inventory — create separate product listings or use tags to distinguish them

Reducing Human Error in Fulfillment

Human error in fulfillment — wrong item shipped, wrong size packed, wrong address used — is inevitable when volume is high and the process is not systematized. Every error costs money (reshipping, returns) and trust (customer experience). The goal is not zero errors — it is a system that catches errors before they leave the warehouse.

Error Type	How It Happens	System Fix
Wrong item shipped	Picker grabs similar item without verifying SKU	Barcode scanning at pick and pack — verify SKU before sealing
Wrong size packed	Multiple sizes look identical in poly bags	Label every poly bag with size before packing — scan to confirm
Wrong address	Address copied incorrectly or customer entered error	Shopify prints address directly on label — never manually copy addresses
Missing item in multi-item order	Rushed packing, items not counted before sealing	Printed packing slip in every order — check each item off before sealing
Duplicate shipment	Order fulfilled twice — manual and automated	Set order status to 'fulfilled' immediately after shipping — prevents second fulfillment

Error Type	How It Happens	System Fix
Damaged item shipped	Defective item not caught before packing	Quality check every item before it goes into a bag — especially after bulk orders arrive

The most impactful single change I made to reduce fulfillment errors was implementing a printed packing slip inside every order. Each packing slip lists every item in the order with the size and quantity. Before the package is sealed, every item is checked against the slip. That one habit eliminated most of the wrong-item and missing-item errors we were experiencing.

Technology That Helps

- Shopify's built-in inventory tracking — free, real-time, syncs with your store automatically
- Stocky by Shopify — free inventory management app for purchase orders and stock transfers
- Linnworks or Skubana — for brands selling on multiple platforms simultaneously — syncs inventory across Shopify, Amazon, Etsy, and more
- ShipStation or ShipBob — for higher-volume brands — adds barcode scanning, batch fulfillment, and error-checking workflows
- Barcode scanner — a basic USB or Bluetooth barcode scanner paired with Shopify's mobile app creates a scan-to-verify workflow at minimal cost

What to Do When You Do Oversell

Despite your best systems, it will occasionally happen. The way you handle it determines the outcome.

- Contact the customer immediately — within hours, not days. Do not wait until the shipment is due.
- Be honest — tell them exactly what happened. Customers respect honesty significantly more than excuses.
- Offer meaningful options — a full refund, a wait for restock with a discount for the inconvenience, or a comparable alternative
- Compensate generously — a store credit or discount on a future order acknowledges the disruption to their experience
- Fix the system — every oversell event should trigger a process review. Why did it happen? What needs to change?

The Lesson

Overselling is a systems problem. Human error is a systems problem. Most operational failures are not failures of effort — they are failures of process. Build the process.

Document it. Train to it. The brand that runs on systems instead of memory scales without breaking.

Motivation

One packing slip. One inventory buffer. One weekly count. These small habits prevent the errors that cost you customers and credibility. Engineer your operations the same way you engineer your product.

CHAPTER 53 — Product Photography — How to Shoot Your Brand With a Phone

Great product photography is not about having the most expensive camera. It is about understanding light, composition, and context — and having the patience to do it right. The brands that consistently produce compelling product imagery are not always the ones with the biggest budgets. They are the ones who understand that the photograph is the first version of the product the customer sees, and it needs to be good enough to sell.

When you cannot afford a professional photographer for every product — and in the beginning, you often cannot — the ability to photograph your own product at a high level is a skill that directly impacts your revenue. A great photo on a bad product will not save the sale. But a bad photo on a great product will definitely lose it.

Light — The Most Important Variable in Photography

Nothing matters more in product photography than light. The right light makes an average composition look great. The wrong light makes a perfect composition look amateur. And the best light is free.

- Natural window light is your best tool — position your product near a large window with indirect sunlight (not direct sun, which creates harsh shadows)
- Golden hour — the hour after sunrise and the hour before sunset — produces the warmest, most cinematic light available without any equipment
- Overcast days are ideal for outdoor shooting — clouds act as a giant diffuser, creating even, soft light with no harsh shadows
- Avoid mixed light sources — overhead fluorescent combined with window light creates uneven color casts that are difficult to correct in editing
- If shooting indoors without natural light, use a continuous LED light panel with a softbox diffuser — a basic setup costs \$50–\$100 and produces consistent results

The Three Types of Product Shots Every Brand Needs

Shot Type	What It Shows	Best Setting	Purpose
Flat lay	Product alone — clean, detail-focused	White or textured neutral background	Website product page — customer sees exactly what they are buying
On-model	Product worn — fit, proportion, styling	Real location or clean studio	Shows the product in context — how it actually looks on a person
Lifestyle	Product in a real environment or activity	Outdoor, urban, authentic setting	Brand content — communicates the world the product belongs to

You need all three. Flat lays for product detail. On-model for fit and proportion. Lifestyle for brand identity and content. A product launch without all three is missing information that customers need to make a purchase decision.

iPhone Settings for Product Photography

- Turn off Live Photo — it adds motion you do not want and increases file size
- Use Portrait mode for close-up product shots — creates depth of field that separates product from background
- Use the 1x lens in good light — the wide lens distorts proportions. Step back and crop rather than zoom digitally.
- Lock exposure and focus — tap and hold on the product in your frame until the AE/AF lock appears. This prevents the camera from re-exposing as you shoot.
- Shoot in RAW or HEIF format for maximum editing flexibility — set in Camera Settings → Formats
- Use a tripod for flat lays — even slight movement creates inconsistency across a product line
- Shoot multiple angles every time — front, back, side, close-up detail, label/tag detail

Editing — The Difference Between Good and Great

- Lightroom Mobile (free) — the best mobile editing app for product photography. Adjust exposure, white balance, contrast, and color with precision.
- VSCO — good for consistent filter presets across a product line — creates a cohesive feed aesthetic
- Snapseed — free, powerful, good for selective adjustments and healing tool to remove distractions

- Adobe Photoshop Express — mobile version of Photoshop — useful for background removal and advanced corrections

Keep your editing consistent across a product line. If all your workshirt photos have the same white balance, exposure, and color treatment, the collection looks intentional and professional on your website. If every photo looks different, the page looks like a marketplace, not a brand.

The Lesson

A customer cannot touch your product before they buy it. The photograph is their hands-on experience. Make it accurate, make it flattering, and make it feel like the brand you are building.

Motivation

Learn to shoot your own product at a high level. It is a skill that pays for itself every time you use it. The best brand photography often comes from the brand owner who cares more about the image than anyone else does.

CHAPTER 54 — What to Do When You Go Viral

Most brand owners spend their time worrying about not enough people seeing their brand. Very few prepare for the opposite problem — what happens when too many people see it at once. A viral moment is one of the most exciting and simultaneously most dangerous things that can happen to an independent fashion brand. If you are ready for it, it changes your trajectory permanently. If you are not, it can damage your reputation in ways that are difficult to recover from.

Going viral does not always mean a post with millions of views. It means a sudden, unexpected spike in traffic and demand that your systems were not calibrated to handle. An athlete wearing your brand in a high-visibility moment. A post that gets picked up by a larger account. A collaboration announcement that resonates beyond your existing audience. Any of these can send more traffic to your store in 24 hours than you normally see in a month.

The Problems That Viral Moments Create

Problem	What Happens	How to Prepare
Website crashes	Traffic overwhelms Shopify server capacity	Shopify handles most spikes — but test your store speed and optimize images before any major announcement
Inventory sells out instantly	Every unit gone in minutes — you cannot fulfill the demand	Set inventory limits per customer, have a back-in-stock notification ready, consider a waitlist

Problem	What Happens	How to Prepare
Overselling	Orders placed exceed inventory available	Inventory buffer, Shopify inventory tracking on, continue selling OFF
Fulfillment backlog	More orders than you can pack and ship in your normal timeline	Have a surge plan — additional help, extended hours, clear communication to customers
Customer service overwhelmed	Hundreds of emails, DMs, and inquiries at once	Prepare auto-responders, FAQ page updated, prioritize communication
Copycats and knockoffs	Other brands copy the product that went viral	Document your designs, have your trademark filed, move fast on the next iteration

How to Prepare Before It Happens

You cannot predict exactly when a viral moment will come. But you can make sure your infrastructure is ready to handle one at any time.

- Keep your Shopify store speed optimized — compress all product images, remove unused apps, use a fast theme
- Always have inventory buffer stock available — the brands that run completely out with no path to restock lose the momentum
- Have a back-in-stock notification system active at all times — capture demand even when you cannot fulfill it immediately
- Know your fulfillment capacity ceiling — how many orders can you pack and ship per day? Know the number before you need it.
- Have a surge communication plan — a drafted email template for 'due to unexpected demand, your order may be delayed' that you can send within hours
- Have a waitlist or pre-order mechanism ready — when you sell out, direct overflow traffic somewhere productive

How to Handle It While It Is Happening

When demand spikes unexpectedly, the first 30 minutes of your response determines the outcome. Here is what to do immediately:

- Check your inventory levels in real time — are you at risk of overselling? Reduce available inventory or pause the listing if needed
- Post on your social media acknowledging the moment — 'we see you, we're working as fast as we can' communicates that a real person is behind the brand

- Update your shipping timeline on the store — add a banner or announcement bar with realistic fulfillment times
- Set up or activate back-in-stock notifications immediately for anything that sells out
- Do not run ads into a stock-out — paying to send traffic to a sold-out product wastes money and frustrates customers
- Document everything — content from the moment, customer reactions, screenshots. This is your brand story.

How to Capitalize on the Moment After

A viral moment brings a wave of new people to your brand. Most of them will not purchase on the first visit — but they are aware now. What you do in the 30 days following a viral moment determines how many of those new people become actual customers.

- Capture emails during the spike — make sure your Klaviyo popup is active and the back-in-stock notification is collecting email addresses
- Retarget the traffic — anyone who visited your store during the spike is a warm audience for retargeting ads
- Restock fast — the faster you can come back in stock after a sellout, the more of that demand you capture before it moves on
- Create follow-up content — ride the momentum with behind-the-scenes, restock announcements, and gratitude content
- Reference the moment in your brand story — a viral moment is social proof. Use it.

The Lesson

A viral moment without infrastructure is a missed opportunity. A viral moment with infrastructure is a turning point. You cannot control when it comes. You can control whether you are ready.

Motivation

Build for the spike before it happens. When it comes — and it will — your systems will handle it while you focus on capitalizing on the momentum.

CHAPTER 55 — Business Insurance — Protecting What You Built

Insurance is the chapter everyone skips until they wish they had not. A customer claims your product caused a skin reaction. A package gets lost with $2,000 worth of inventory inside. A fire damages your warehouse. Someone trips and falls at your pop-up. Without the right insurance, any of these events becomes a personal financial crisis. With the right insurance, they become manageable business events.

This is not a glamorous topic. But the brand owners who build for the long term treat risk management as seriously as they treat product development. You cannot build a lasting brand if a single incident can wipe out everything you created.

Types of Insurance Every Brand Owner Should Know

Insurance Type	What It Covers	Who Needs It	Approximate Cost
General Liability	Third-party bodily injury or property damage — customer injured at pop-up, product causes harm	Every brand owner — especially if you do pop-ups or have a physical location	\$400–\$1,500/year
Product Liability	Claims that your product caused harm — skin reaction, injury from wearing the product	Any brand selling physical products — often bundled with general liability	Included in GL or \$300–\$800/year standalone
Commercial Property	Damage to your inventory, equipment, and business property — fire, theft, water damage	Anyone with a warehouse, studio, or significant inventory value	\$500–\$2,000/year depending on coverage amount
Business Owner's Policy (BOP)	Bundles general liability + commercial property — most cost-effective for small businesses	Most independent brand owners — best value for comprehensive coverage	\$750–\$2,500/year
Commercial Auto	Vehicles used for business — delivery, pop-up transport, manufacturer runs	Anyone using a personal vehicle regularly for business purposes	Varies — add-on to personal auto or separate policy
Cyber Liability	Data breaches, customer data exposure — especially relevant for e-commerce	Any brand storing customer payment or personal information	\$500–\$2,000/year

Where to Get It

- Next Insurance — purpose-built for small businesses and e-commerce, fast online quotes, well-reviewed for independent brand owners
- Hiscox — strong for product liability and general liability, good for creative and fashion businesses

- Thimble — flexible policies including by-the-day coverage for pop-up events specifically
- Your existing personal insurance carrier — ask about business add-ons to your existing policies
- A local independent insurance broker — can compare multiple carriers and find the best combination for your specific situation

For pop-up events specifically — many venues now require a certificate of insurance before you can set up. Thimble allows you to purchase event-specific coverage by the day, which is cost-effective if you only do a few events per year.

The Lesson

You spent years building something real. Insurance is what protects it from being taken away by a single incident you could not predict. The cost of a Business Owner's Policy is less than most brand owners spend on ads in a month.

Motivation

Get covered before you need it. The brand owner who has insurance and never uses it paid for peace of mind. The brand owner who needed it and did not have it paid a much higher price.

CHAPTER 56 — Continuous Improvement — The Philosophy That Keeps You Winning

There is a concept in engineering called kaizen — a Japanese philosophy of continuous, incremental improvement. It is the idea that small improvements made consistently over time compound into transformative results. It is the principle that Toyota built one of the most reliable manufacturing operations in the world on. And it is the philosophy that, more than any single strategy or tactic, determines which brands last and which ones peak and fade.

Every system you build, every product you make, every process you run — none of them are finished. They are all drafts. The brand owner who treats their current operation as the best it can ever be has already started falling behind. The brand owner who looks at everything they do and asks 'how can this be better?' is the one who is still building five years from now.

What Continuous Improvement Actually Looks Like

Continuous improvement is not a dramatic overhaul. It is a relentless series of small upgrades that individually feel minor but collectively transform the brand. Here is what it looks like in practice:

Area	What Continuous Improvement Looks Like
Product	Every new sample is better than the last. You refine the fit, the fabric, the construction with each production run.
Photography	Every shoot teaches you something. Better locations, better lighting, better direction on each one.
Customer service	Every complaint teaches you something. Fix the source, not just the symptom.
Fulfillment	Every error gets a system fix. Every bottleneck gets a process improvement.
Marketing	Every campaign teaches you what works. You test, measure, and apply the learning.
Manufacturer relationship	Every order is a conversation about what could be better next time — quality, timing, communication.
Website	Every month review conversion rate, page speed, and customer feedback. Make one improvement.
Financial management	Every quarter review margins, expenses, and reinvestment allocation. Adjust what needs adjusting.

The Review Habit — Building Improvement Into Your Schedule

Continuous improvement does not happen spontaneously. It requires deliberate review cycles where you examine what is working, what is not, and what can be made better. Build these into your calendar before you need them.

- Weekly — review orders, fulfillment accuracy, customer service tickets, inventory levels. Catch operational problems early.
- Monthly — review revenue, margins, ad performance, email metrics, website conversion rate. Look for trends not just snapshots.
- Quarterly — review product performance, manufacturer relationships, team performance, financial health. Make structural decisions.
- Annually — review the full brand. Where did it grow? Where did it stagnate? What does the next year need to look like?

The brands that do these reviews consistently are the ones that compound. They do not just react to problems — they anticipate them. They do not just repeat what worked — they improve on it. They are always slightly better than they were the last time.

The Mindset of the Continuous Improver

The most important shift required for continuous improvement is releasing the ego investment in your current way of doing things. The product that you launched and loved — it can be better. The system that you built and were proud of — it can be more efficient. The strategy that worked last quarter — it may need to evolve for this one.

Attachment to the current version of anything is the enemy of improvement. The brands that stay great are the ones whose founders can look at something they built and say: this was excellent for where we were, and here is how we make it even better for where we are going.

Criticism — from customers, from team members, from your own honest self-assessment — is not a threat to the brand. It is the fuel for improvement. The brand owner who receives feedback defensively never uses it. The brand owner who receives it openly and acts on it keeps getting better.

Continuous Improvement as a Competitive Advantage

In an industry where most brands peak early and fade, the brand that improves consistently is almost impossible to catch. You may start behind a competitor in budget, audience, or resources. But if you improve faster than they do — if your product gets better every season, your marketing gets sharper every quarter, your operations get more efficient every month — the gap closes. And then it reverses.

The long way is the shortcut. Consistent improvement over time beats sporadic brilliance every time. The brand that was a little better this month than last month, every month, for five years — that brand looks like overnight success to everyone watching from the outside.

That is not luck. That is engineering.

The Lesson

You will never be finished. The product can always be better. The process can always be more efficient. The brand can always be more compelling. That is not a failure. That is the nature of building something worth building.

Motivation

Commit to continuous improvement. Make it a habit, not an event. The brand that gets 1% better every week is 52% better by the end of the year. Do that for five years and you are in a different category entirely. That is how you build something that lasts.

PART V — SCALING WITHOUT BREAKING

How to grow without losing control.

CHAPTER 57 — Financial Literacy & Working Capital

Growth does not expose a lack of talent. It exposes a lack of financial control. Revenue is not profit. Cash flow is not income. Sales do not equal stability.

The Control Check — Know These Numbers Always

- How much money is coming in this month
- How much money is going out this month
- What production obligations are upcoming
- What the business can realistically afford
- Monthly overhead (rent, employees, software, insurance)
- Cost per product including all fees
- Upcoming bulk order deposits and balances

The Lesson

Money stops controlling you when you understand it. Financial literacy creates options. Options create confidence.

Motivation

The goal is not fast growth. The goal is stable growth.

CHAPTER 58 — What to Do With Profits

Early profits are not rewards. They are fuel. The smartest early move is simple: put the money back into the business.

- Sampling and new product development
- Inventory for proven sellers
- Marketing and content creation
- Better materials and construction
- Systems and tools that save time
- Warehouse and fulfillment improvements

Short-term gratification kills long-term companies. Reinvesting today buys freedom tomorrow.

CHAPTER 59 — Your First Release Is Data

Your first drop is not a final judgment. It is information. Do not rush to conclusions — learn, adjust, and improve.

- What sold (and what did not)
- Customer feedback and sizing issues
- Product refinement opportunities
- Better targeting for next release
- Timing and demand patterns

Feedback is not failure. It is direction. There is always a way to make a way.

CHAPTER 60 — Advertising as a System

Ads are not luck. They are levers. A strong ad system is built on four levers:

Lever	What It Controls
TIME	Let ads run 30+ days — algorithms need time to learn
TARGETING	Age, location, interests — pay for relevance, not volume
TRAFFIC TEMPERATURE	Cold = discovery, Retargeting = conversion
CREATIVE	Change one variable at a time to learn what works

The Lesson

Do not interrupt learning because of impatience. The algorithm rewards patience, not panic.

Motivation

Ads stop feeling expensive and start feeling predictable when you build systems.

CHAPTER 61 — Influencers as Ambassadors

Influencers are not just marketing tools. When used correctly, they are distribution partners.

The Ambassador Model

- Each ambassador receives a personal 10% discount code
- The customer gets 10% off their order
- The ambassador earns 10% commission on every sale generated

- The brand only pays when revenue is created — no wasted spend

---

The Lesson

Influencers become powerful when they are invested, not rented.

Motivation

Give them a reason to build with you. When creators win with you, your brand grows beyond ads.

CHAPTER 62 — Scaling Without Losing Control

Not every season is meant for expansion. Some seasons are meant for stabilization. Growth without structure creates pressure. Pressure without clarity creates mistakes.

- Pause new drops to strengthen systems
- Reduce inventory risk
- Slow marketing spend
- Reorganize operations
- Protect quality as volume increases

The Lesson

Control outlasts speed.

Motivation

The goal is not to grow fast. The goal is to grow correctly.

CHAPTER 63 — Sustaining the Brand

Hype is temporary. Structure is permanent. Attention can spike overnight. But only systems keep a brand alive when attention fades.

- Prioritize repeat customers over viral moments
- Protect quality as volume increases
- Maintain identity instead of trend chasing
- Reinforce systems during slow seasons
- Make decisions for years ahead, not weeks

The Lesson

Attention starts brands. Structure keeps them alive.

Motivation

You do not need to be everywhere. You need to be reliable.

CHAPTER 64 — Legacy Thinking

Your last name is the real brand. Every decision shapes perception. Every shortcut writes a story. Every standard you keep becomes visible over time. What you tolerate becomes culture. What you repeat becomes legacy.

- Will this decision still make sense years from now?
- Does this align with who I want this brand to represent?
- Would I be proud of this if my name is attached to it?

The Lesson

You are not just building a business. You are building a reputation.

Motivation

Build something you can stand behind long after the trend passes.

The Lesson

You are not just building a business. You are building a reputation.

Motivation

Build something you can stand behind long after the trend passes.

PART VII — BECOMING THE BUSINESS OWNER

The shift from making products to running a company.

Most people who start fashion brands are great at the creative side. They know what looks good. They know what they want to make. But longevity does not come from great taste alone. It comes from becoming the kind of business owner who can sustain great taste. This part of the book is about that transition.

Whether you are just starting out or have been running your brand for years — this is the section that separates the ones who last from the ones who peak early.

CHAPTER 65 — The Owner Mindset vs The Designer Mindset

There is a difference between a designer and a business owner. A designer thinks about what to create. A business owner thinks about what the business needs. Both matter — but only one of them keeps the lights on.

Most people who start fashion brands start as designers. That is natural. The problem is that many of them never make the transition. They stay in designer mode even as the business grows — and that is where things break down.

What the Shift Looks Like in Practice

Designer Mindset	Owner Mindset
'I want to make this product'	'Does this product serve the business right now?'
'This design looks great'	'Will this design perform at scale?'
'I'll figure out pricing later'	'Margin is built into every decision from the start'
'I'll handle that when it happens'	'I have a system for when that happens'
'I do everything myself'	'What can I delegate, automate, or eliminate?'
'Sales are up, we are doing great'	'What are our margins, costs, and runway?'
'I want more followers'	'I want more repeat customers'

The designer in you is an asset. Do not kill it. But the owner in you is what the business needs to survive. Learn to switch between the two deliberately — put the designer hat on when you are creating, and the owner hat on when you are running.

The most dangerous phase for any brand is right after the first success. That is when the designer says 'let's make more' and the owner says 'let's understand why that worked first.' Listen to the owner. The designer's enthusiasm without the owner's discipline is the most common reason brands fade.

The Lesson

Your creativity got you started. Your discipline will keep you going. The transition from designer to owner is not a loss — it is a promotion.

Motivation

You are not giving up the creative side. You are building the infrastructure that protects it.

CHAPTER 66 — Building a Business That Runs Without You

If your business stops when you stop, you do not own a business. You own a job. The goal is to build systems so strong that the business can operate whether you are present or not.

This does not mean you remove yourself entirely. It means you build documentation, processes, and tools that reduce your dependence on being hands-on for every single thing. When you can step away for a week and come back to a functioning operation, you have built something real.

Start With Documentation

Every repeatable process in your business should be written down. Not in your head. Written down. A Standard Operating Procedure (SOP) is just a step-by-step document that explains how to do a specific task. You do not need fancy software. A Google Doc works fine.

- How to process an order
- How to respond to a customer complaint
- How to communicate with a manufacturer about a revision
- How to prepare a product for launch
- How to reconcile monthly financials

When something is documented, anyone can follow it. That means you can train someone to help you, and the quality stays consistent even when you are not involved.

The Three Questions Before Every Task

Before you do any recurring task, ask: Can this be automated? Can this be delegated? Does this actually need to happen?

Automation handles the repetitive: email flows, order confirmations, back-in-stock notifications, social media scheduling. Delegation handles the operational: customer service, packaging, content editing. Elimination handles the time-wasters: unnecessary meetings, tasks that produce no outcome, processes that exist out of habit not necessity.

Your time as the owner is most valuable when it is spent on vision, relationships, and decisions that only you can make. Everything else is a system waiting to be built.

The Lesson

A business that runs without you is not a passive income fantasy. It is the result of documented systems, trusted people, and deliberate automation built over time.

Motivation

Start building the version of your business that does not need you to survive every day. That is how you grow.

CHAPTER 67 — Understanding Your Numbers Like a CEO

You do not need to be an accountant to run a great brand. But you do need to understand the numbers that tell you whether your business is healthy or bleeding. Most creative business owners avoid this. The ones who last do not.

Here are the numbers that matter most — explained plainly.

The Numbers Every Brand Owner Must Know

Number	What It Tells You	Why It Matters
Revenue	Total money coming in from sales	Starting point — but not the full picture
Cost of Goods Sold (COGS)	What it costs to make what you sell	Fabric, manufacturing, shipping to you
Gross Profit	Revenue minus COGS	What you actually made before expenses
Gross Margin %	Gross profit divided by revenue	Target 50%+ for a healthy fashion brand
Operating Expenses	Rent, software, ads, salaries, fees	What it costs to run the business
Net Profit	What's left after everything	The real score
Cash Flow	When money comes in vs goes out	Cash flow problems kill profitable brands
Average Order Value (AOV)	Average amount per purchase	Raising AOV grows revenue without more customers
Customer Lifetime Value (LTV)	Total revenue from one customer over time	The most underused number in fashion
Return Rate	% of orders returned	High returns signal a product or expectation problem

The One Financial Habit That Changes Everything

Look at your numbers every week. Not once a quarter. Not when tax season comes. Every week. It takes 15 minutes and it will catch problems before they become crises. A sudden drop in conversion rate, a spike in return rate, an unusually high ad spend with no corresponding revenue increase — these are visible in the numbers before they become painful in the bank account.

Use a simple spreadsheet if you are early stage. Use accounting software like QuickBooks or Wave when you scale. But whatever you use — look at it regularly and understand what you are seeing.

The Lesson

The best fashion brands in the world are run by people who love the product and respect the numbers equally. You cannot scale what you cannot measure.

Motivation

Start treating your financials like product feedback. They are telling you something every single week.

CHAPTER 68 — Customer Retention Is Your Real Business

Acquisition gets you customers. Retention builds a brand. Most fashion brands spend 90% of their energy getting new customers and almost nothing keeping the ones they already have. That is backwards.

A customer who buys once is a transaction. A customer who buys three times is a fan. A customer who buys every drop and tells their friends is an asset. The difference between those three outcomes is almost entirely determined by what happens after the first purchase.

The Real Numbers Behind Retention

- Acquiring a new customer costs 5–7x more than retaining an existing one
- A 5% increase in retention can increase profits by 25–95%
- Repeat customers spend 67% more than first-time buyers on average
- Your email and SMS list is your retention engine — protect it

What Retention Actually Looks Like

Retention is not just sending emails. It is the entire experience after purchase. The shipping speed. The packaging quality. The product living up to what was promised. The follow-up that feels personal, not automated. The next drop announcement that makes them feel like an insider.

Your private room — your email list, your SMS list, your repeat buyers — is the most valuable asset your brand has. Social media followers can disappear overnight when an algorithm changes. Your email list is yours. Your SMS list is yours. Protect those relationships like the business depends on them. Because it does.

First Purchase Experience	What It Creates
Fast, clean shipping	Trust in your operations
Quality packaging	Perceived premium value
Product matches expectations	Credibility and confidence
Post-purchase email sequence	Connection and anticipation
Early access to next drop	Identity — they feel like part of something

First Purchase Experience	What It Creates
Review request at the right time	Social proof for future buyers

---

The Lesson

Your best marketing is a customer who comes back and brings someone with them. That only happens when the experience earns it.

Motivation

Stop chasing new customers at the expense of the ones you already won. Retention is where the real money is.

CHAPTER 69 — When to Hire, Outsource, or Do It Yourself

One of the most common mistakes growing brand owners make is holding on to everything too long. Doing everything yourself felt like control in the beginning. At a certain point, it becomes the ceiling.

The goal is not to do everything. The goal is to make sure everything gets done well. Those are two very different things.

The Decision Framework

Do It Yourself When...	Outsource When...	Hire When...
You are learning the skill	The skill is not your strength	You need someone consistently
The task defines the brand	Speed matters more than learning	Volume requires a dedicated person
No one else can do it yet	The cost is justified by the time saved	The role drives revenue or protects it
You are early and lean	Quality requires a specialist	You are ready to build a team

The Right Order of Hiring

Most brand owners hire in the wrong order. They hire for the tasks they hate before they hire for the tasks that grow the business. Here is a better sequence:

- First: Automate what can be automated (email flows, order notifications, social scheduling)
- Second: Outsource what requires skill but not ongoing presence (photography, graphic design, accounting)

- Third: Part-time help for operational tasks (packaging, fulfillment, customer service)
- Fourth: Full-time hire when a role clearly drives revenue and cannot be covered any other way

Hiring too early creates overhead that kills cash flow. Hiring too late creates a ceiling that limits growth. The answer is always: systematize first, then add people to support the system.

The Lesson

Your time is the most expensive resource in your business. Spend it on the things only you can do. Build systems and people around everything else.

Motivation

The brands that scale are not built by one person doing everything. They are built by one person building the right team at the right time.

CHAPTER 70 — Protecting What You Build

You can build a great brand and lose it if you do not protect it. Protection is not paranoia. It is preparation. The brands that last are the ones whose owners understood that intellectual property, contracts, and legal structure are not optional — they are infrastructure.

Trademark Your Brand

A trademark protects your brand name and logo from being used by others in your industry. Without a trademark, anyone can legally use a name similar to yours and you will have limited recourse. The filing process through the USPTO (United States Patent and Trademark Office) costs a few hundred dollars and takes several months. It is worth every penny.

- File your brand name as a trademark — this is the most important one
- File your logo separately if it is distinctive enough to stand alone
- Search the USPTO database before you finalize a name to avoid conflicts
- Use the ™ symbol before registration is approved, ® after

Contracts Are Not Just for Big Companies

Every collaboration, partnership, and significant business relationship should have a written agreement. A simple email thread is not a contract. A contract defines who owns what, who gets paid what, what happens if someone does not deliver, and how disputes are resolved.

- Collaboration agreements — who owns the IP, how revenue is split
- Photographer and creative agreements — who owns the images
- Manufacturer agreements — quality standards, revision rights, confidentiality

- Vendor and supplier agreements — pricing, minimums, timelines

You do not need an expensive lawyer for every agreement. Templates exist for most standard situations. But get something in writing before money and work exchange hands.

Separate Personal From Business — Always

Your LLC protects your personal assets from business liabilities. But only if you treat the business like a separate entity. That means a separate bank account, separate credit card, separate finances. The moment you commingle personal and business money, you weaken your legal protection. Keep them completely separate from day one.

The Lesson

What you build has value. Protect it like it does. The cost of protection is always less than the cost of losing what you built.

Motivation

You did not come this far to have it taken from you. Build the legal infrastructure that keeps your work yours.

CHAPTER 71 — The Slow Season Is Not Your Enemy

Every brand has slow seasons. Revenue dips. Traffic drops. The feed gets quiet. Most brand owners panic during these periods. The ones who last use them.

The slow season is not a sign that something is wrong. It is a signal that you have time to fix what is not right. When business is fast, you are reacting. When business is slow, you can be intentional.

What to Do When Things Slow Down

- Audit your store — fix every broken link, outdated policy, missing size chart
- Review your data — what sold, what did not, what sizes keep selling out, what stays on the shelf
- Build your next systems — email flows, SOPs, product documentation
- Develop new products — slow season is when sampling should start for the next busy season
- Strengthen manufacturer relationships — check in, discuss upcoming orders, negotiate better terms
- Invest in content — shoot lookbooks, film brand videos, build creative assets for the next launch
- Study the business — read, learn, analyze competitors, understand your industry better

The brands that dominate their busy seasons built everything during their slow ones. The launch that looks effortless was prepared for months. The drop that sells out in hours was planned in the quiet.

Do not waste the slow season wishing it were busy. Use it to make sure the next busy season is your best one yet.

The Lesson

Slow seasons are not punishments. They are preparation time. The brands that show up strongest are the ones that used the quiet to build.

Motivation

When the noise comes back, you will be ready. That is not luck. That is engineering.

CHAPTER 72 — Collaborations, Partnerships & Growing Your Network

No brand grows alone. Every major brand you respect has been shaped by the relationships behind it — collaborators who pushed the creative, partners who opened doors, a network that amplified the message. Building relationships is not soft work. It is strategic work.

The Right Collaboration Philosophy

A collaboration is not just about exposure. It is about alignment. The best collaborations happen when two brands share the same values, the same customer, or the same vision — and together they can create something neither could create alone.

Before entering any collaboration, ask: Does this brand's audience overlap with mine in a meaningful way? Does this partnership move both brands forward? Is there clear agreement on who owns what and how revenue is split? If the answer to any of those is unclear, slow down.

Collaboration Type	What It Does	When to Pursue It
Brand x Brand co-release	Creates new audience overlap and shared hype	When both brands are aligned in values and audience
Influencer x Brand	Distributes product to a trusted audience	When the influencer's audience is your customer
Artist x Brand	Adds creative credibility and uniqueness	When the art elevates what the product communicates
Event x Brand	Places the brand in a physical space and culture	When the event reaches your target community
Corporate x Brand	Large-scale exposure and legitimate credibility	When the corporation's values align with yours

Building a Network That Compounds

Your network is not your follower count. Your network is the people who would take your call. Photographers, manufacturers, other brand owners, buyers, stylists, event organizers, media contacts — these are the relationships that open doors ads cannot.

Be generous before you need something. Show up for other people's launches. Share knowledge. Give referrals. Buy from brands you respect. The fashion industry is smaller than it looks and your reputation in it travels faster than your product does.

The relationship you build with another brand owner today might become a collaboration that changes your trajectory two years from now. You cannot predict which connection will matter most. You can only show up consistently and build with integrity.

The Lesson

Your network is a long-term asset. It compounds over time the same way money does — the more you invest, the more it returns.

Motivation

Build relationships the same way you build products. With intention, with quality, and with the long game in mind.

PART VI — ENGINEERING WITH AI

How to use artificial intelligence as a business tool, not a shortcut.

CHAPTER 73 — What AI Actually Is for Builders

There is a lot of noise around artificial intelligence. Some people treat it like magic. Some people are afraid of it. Both responses miss the point.

AI is a tool. Like any tool, it is only as powerful as the person using it. A hammer in the wrong hands builds nothing. In the right hands, it builds a house. The same applies here.

For brand builders, AI is not a replacement for thinking. It is an amplifier of thinking. It does not replace your vision, your taste, or your decision-making. It accelerates everything around those things — research, drafting, setup, systems, analysis, communication.

The creators who will dominate the next decade are not the ones who ignore AI and the ones who rely on it blindly. They are the ones who learn to direct it. Who bring their own strategy, their own standards, and their own voice — and use AI to execute faster, cheaper, and smarter.

What AI Can Do for Your Brand Right Now

- Draft legal documents, policies, and contracts in minutes instead of paying a lawyer for hours
- Set up email flows, automations, and customer sequences without a marketing agency
- Research manufacturers, compare platforms, and analyze competition
- Write product descriptions, ad copy, and campaign messaging at scale
- Configure store apps, integrations, and tech tools step by step
- Build systems and infrastructure that used to require an entire team

The Mindset That Makes AI Useful

AI does not know your brand better than you do. It never will. What it knows is process, structure, and language. Your job is to bring the vision. AI's job is to help you execute it.

Think of it the way you think about a manufacturer. You do not let the factory decide what your product looks like. You give them the specs, you review the samples, you approve the final run. AI works the same way. You direct it. You review the output. You decide what stays.

The Lesson

AI is leverage. Leverage multiplies what you already bring. Bring something worth multiplying.

Motivation

The builder who uses AI correctly works like a team of ten. The builder who ignores it competes against one.

CHAPTER 74 — How AI Saved Me Thousands Building This Brand

I want to be specific here, because specificity is where lessons live.

When I was building the infrastructure for Engineered By Dré — the policies, the store setup, the apps, the email systems, the fraud protection — I used AI as my operator. Not as a generator of generic content, but as a collaborator that helped me make real decisions in real time.

What We Built Together

Here is a concrete example. Setting up a brand's legal and operational foundation — Privacy Policy, Terms of Service, Return & Exchange Policy, Shipping Policy, Contact page — typically requires a lawyer, a copywriter, or hours of research. Agencies charge thousands for this kind of setup. With AI, I had all five documents drafted, customized to my specific business, and published on my site in a fraction of the time and at a fraction of the cost.

Each document reflected the actual policies of Engineered By Dré — our 30-day defective window, our 4-6 week custom production timeline, our shipping carriers (USPS, UPS, FedEx, DHL), our Georgia-based operations, our contact email. Not generic templates. Real, brand-specific infrastructure.

The App Infrastructure

Beyond documents, I built out the store's conversion infrastructure with AI guidance. Back In Stock notifications through Kbite — so sold-out products keep capturing demand instead of losing customers permanently. Cross-sell and upsell capabilities through Zoorix — so customers buying a workshirt are shown wallet chains, beanies, and accessories without any manual work. Fraud protection through NoFraud — so orders are reviewed before they ship, preventing chargebacks before they happen instead of fighting them after.

Each of these systems, running together, creates compounding revenue. They work while I sleep. They run without a team. And the setup that might have taken weeks working with agencies was completed in focused sessions working with AI.

The Real Cost Comparison

Task	Agency / Freelancer Cost	With AI Guidance
5 Legal Policy Documents	$500–$2,000	Hours, not dollars

Task	Agency / Freelancer Cost	With AI Guidance
Email Marketing Setup	$1,000–$3,000	Done in one session
Store App Configuration	$500–$1,500	Configured step by step
Fraud Protection Setup	$200–$500	Free app, self-configured
Upsell / Cross-Sell Setup	$300–$800	Guided setup, no agency
Total Estimated Savings	$2,500–$7,800+	Reinvested into the brand

Those are not hypothetical savings. That is money that stayed in the business instead of going to a third party. Money that funded inventory, marketing, and growth.

Beyond Setup: AI as an Ongoing Operator

The value of AI is not just in the one-time setup. It is in the ongoing decisions. When a new app drops and you need to understand whether it is worth installing. When a legal question comes up about a collaboration contract. When you need to draft a response to a difficult customer situation, write a product launch email, or analyze which campaigns are worth scaling.

AI is available at 2 AM when your manufacturer responds. It is available when you are traveling and a store issue comes up. It is available when you need to think through a decision quickly and clearly.

The brands that will win the next decade are not necessarily the ones with the most money or the biggest teams. They are the ones that operate the most efficiently. AI levels that playing field.

The Lesson

Every dollar you save on setup is a dollar you can put into inventory, marketing, or growth. AI is not a shortcut — it is a force multiplier for builders who already know what they are building.

Motivation

Use it. Direct it. Profit from it.

CHAPTER 75 — How AI Built the Store — Klaviyo, Postscript, Reviews & Social Proof

Let me walk you through what the finished store infrastructure looks like — and how each piece was set up with AI as the guide. Because understanding the tools is one thing. Seeing them connected as a system is another.

Klaviyo — The Email Engine

Klaviyo is not just an email platform. It is the central nervous system of your marketing. It tracks every visitor, every purchase, every abandoned cart, every product view — and it lets you automate responses to all of it.

The setup on Engineered By Dré includes a 15% OFF popup that fires once per visitor. Not on every page. Not on every visit. Once. It shows the offer, captures the email, and the teaser tab stays visible so returning visitors can access it again if they want. This one popup runs automatically and builds the private room every single day.

Once someone is on the list, Klaviyo handles what comes next. A welcome sequence introduces them to the brand. An abandoned cart sequence follows up at one hour, 24 hours, and 72 hours if they did not complete their purchase. A post-purchase sequence confirms their order, provides tracking, and asks for a review. A win-back sequence reaches out if someone has not purchased in 60 days. All of this runs without lifting a finger.

Klaviyo Flow	When It Fires	Revenue Impact
Welcome Sequence	Immediately after email signup	Introduces brand, drives first purchase
Abandoned Cart — 1hr	1 hour after cart abandoned	Captures impulse buyers still considering
Abandoned Cart — 24hr	24 hours after cart abandoned	Catches busy buyers who forgot
Abandoned Cart — 72hr	72 hours after cart abandoned	Final reminder with urgency
Post-Purchase	After every completed order	Builds loyalty, asks for review
Win-Back	60 days since last purchase	Recovers lapsed customers with a reason to return
Back In Stock	When inventory restores	Converts customers who already showed intent

The difference between a store that makes sporadic sales and a store that generates consistent revenue is almost always the email system. Sporadic stores rely on people coming back on their own. Consistent stores go get them.

Postscript — The SMS Line

Email converts well. SMS converts better for time-sensitive moments. A text message has a 98% open rate. A limited drop announcement, a back-in-stock alert, a flash sale — these hit different over text than they do over email.

Postscript captures phone numbers at checkout and through opt-in prompts. Once a customer is on the SMS list, they are in the innermost circle of the private room. They get the information first, at the highest priority channel.

The setup is intentional: Postscript handles the urgency plays. Klaviyo handles the relationship plays. Together they cover every stage of the customer relationship — from discovery to loyalty.

Product Reviews — Converting Strangers Into Believers

Reviews are the most powerful trust signal on any product page. A stranger landing on your store does not know you. They cannot feel the fabric. They cannot see the fit in person. What they can see is what other real customers said.

Every product on Engineered By Dré now has a reviews section. This is not decoration — it is conversion infrastructure. A product with 47 five-star reviews converts at a fundamentally different rate than the same product with no social proof. The quality of the product stays the same. The customer's confidence changes completely.

The review system is automated. Klaviyo's post-purchase flow requests a review at the right moment — after the customer has received and had time to wear the product. That timing matters. Asking too early gets no response. Asking at the right moment gets real feedback that converts future buyers.

Without Reviews	With Reviews
Customer has to trust the brand alone	Customer sees proof from real buyers
Hesitation is harder to overcome	Hesitation is pre-answered by others' experience
First-time buyers feel risk	First-time buyers feel validated
Conversion depends entirely on visuals and copy	Conversion is supported by social proof at every scroll

Instagram Photos on the Website — The Community Section

The 'Made by us, Shared by you' section on the Engineered By Dré homepage does something reviews alone cannot do — it shows the brand alive in the real world. Not on a model. Not in a studio. On real people, in real moments, captured and shared organically.

This section pulls real customer and community photos from Instagram directly onto the website. When a visitor sees a product they are considering being worn by someone who looks like them, doing something they relate to, the connection between interest and intent closes fast.

Social proof comes in layers. Reviews tell you what people think. Community photos show you how people live in the brand. Both are needed. One speaks to the mind. The other speaks to identity.

The setup: a curated feed of real community content, updated automatically, embedded on the homepage where first impressions form. No manual updates. No team required. It runs and evolves on its own.

How All of It Works Together

Individually, each of these tools adds value. Together, they create a system where almost no one leaves the store empty-handed.

- Visitor arrives from an ad or organic post
- Klaviyo popup captures email — they are now in the private room
- They browse a product — cross-sell shows them what pairs with it
- Community photos show real people wearing it — identity connects
- Reviews confirm others loved it — hesitation dissolves
- They add to cart — Zoorix prompts a related item in the cart
- They check out — NoFraud clears the order before it ships
- Post-purchase email confirms the order and sets expectations
- Review request arrives at the right moment — they leave a review
- Next drop arrives — they get the Klaviyo email and the Postscript text
- They come back. And they bring people with them.

This is not a complicated system. It is a connected one. And connection is what converts.

The Lesson

Every tool in this stack was set up intentionally, not randomly. The store was engineered the same way the products were — with a clear purpose for every piece.

Motivation

Build the machine before you send the traffic. The machine is what turns attention into revenue.

CHAPTER 76 — AI as a Daily Business Tool

AI is most powerful when it becomes part of your daily operation — not a tool you use once to set something up and forget.

Daily Uses That Compound Over Time

- Writing and reviewing customer service responses that maintain brand voice
- Drafting product descriptions that convert — specific, sensory, and brand-aligned
- Generating ad copy variations to test across platforms
- Researching new manufacturers, fabrics, or materials before committing
- Analyzing your store data and identifying patterns in what sells
- Preparing for negotiations — what to ask for, what to expect, what to walk away from

- Staying current on platform changes, algorithm updates, and industry developments

What AI Cannot Replace

Your eye. Your taste. Your relationships. Your brand's specific identity and the culture you have built around it. AI can help you write a product description. It cannot tell you whether the product is worth building. AI can help you set up an email flow. It cannot replace the trust you have built with your customer base over years of consistency.

Use AI to handle the things that do not require your taste. That frees your taste for the things that do.

The Lesson

The best operators use every available tool. AI is the most powerful tool available to independent builders right now.

Motivation

The question is not whether to use it. The question is whether you will learn to use it better than everyone else.

CHAPTER 77 — The Engineer's AI Toolkit

Here are the tools worth knowing and using:

Tool	Best Use for Brand Builders
Claude (Anthropic)	Deep reasoning, document drafting, store setup, strategy, long-form writing
ChatGPT (OpenAI)	Quick research, brainstorming, content generation, customer service drafts
Midjourney / DALL-E	Mockup visualization, cover art concepts, mood boarding
Perplexity	Real-time research with sourced answers — manufacturer research, market data
Notion AI	Organizing business operations, SOPs, content calendars
Klaviyo AI	Email subject line optimization, send time prediction, segment suggestions

You do not need all of these. You need the ones that solve real problems in your current stage of building. Start with one. Master it. Add others as your needs grow.

The Lesson

A builder with the right tools outperforms a builder with the wrong team.

Motivation

Engineer your workflow the same way you engineer your product. Intentionally.

PART VIII — THE REAL STUFF NOBODY TALKS ABOUT

The chapters most business books skip.

Every business book will tell you how to build. Very few will tell you what it actually feels like to build. This part is the one I wish someone had given me before I started. Not the tactics — the truth. The financial realities. The emotional weight. The customer moments that test your character. The seasons that shake your belief. And how to come back from all of it.

CHAPTER 78 — Email Marketing Is Your Most Valuable Asset

Your social media following is borrowed. The platform owns it. Instagram can change its algorithm tomorrow and your reach can drop by 80% overnight. TikTok can be banned in a country. A post can be suppressed for reasons you will never understand. None of that is in your control.

Your email list is yours. Nobody can take it from you. No algorithm decides who sees your message. When you send an email to your list, it lands in every inbox — every single one. That is a direct line to your customer that no social platform can offer and no competitor can interrupt.

Most brand owners treat email as an afterthought. They build social followings of tens of thousands and email lists of a few hundred. That is backwards. The email list is the business. The social following is the funnel that feeds it.

Why Email Converts Better Than Social

Social Media Post	Email
Seen by 3–10% of followers organically	Delivered to 100% of subscribers
Algorithm controls distribution	You control distribution
Easy to scroll past	Opened with intent — they chose to open it
Platform can remove or suppress	Yours permanently
Average conversion rate: 0.5–1%	Average conversion rate: 2–5%+
Built on borrowed land	Built on owned land

Building Your List

Every tool you use to capture emails is an investment in your most valuable asset. The Klaviyo popup with a 15% off offer. The SMS capture at checkout. The back in stock notification. The post-purchase review request. Every one of these touchpoints adds someone to a list that you own and can reach directly for the rest of the brand's life.

Treat list growth like product development. It requires intention and consistency. A brand with 500 highly engaged email subscribers will outperform a brand with 50,000 social followers and no list — every time.

The Email Flows That Generate Revenue on Autopilot

Email marketing is not just sending newsletters. The real revenue comes from automated flows — sequences that fire automatically based on what a customer does or does not do.

Flow	When It Fires	What It Does
Welcome Sequence	Immediately after signup	Introduces the brand, builds connection, drives first purchase
Abandoned Cart — 1hr	1 hour after abandonment	Catches impulse buyers who got distracted
Abandoned Cart — 24hr	24 hours after abandonment	Catches the busy buyer who meant to come back
Abandoned Cart — 72hr	72 hours after abandonment	Final reminder — create urgency
Post-Purchase	After every order	Confirms order, sets shipping expectations, builds loyalty
Review Request	7–14 days after delivery	Asks for a review at the right moment
Win-Back	60 days since last purchase	Re-engages customers who have gone quiet
Back In Stock	When inventory returns	Converts customers who already showed buying intent
Drop Announcement	Before every launch	Warms up the private room before the public sees it

These flows run while you sleep. While you are at a pop-up. While you are sampling a new product. While you are on a plane. The brand is generating revenue and building relationships without you lifting a finger — because you built the system.

How to Write Emails That Get Opened

- Subject line is everything — write it last, after you know what the email actually says
- Keep it short — most people read email on their phone, one scroll should cover it
- Write like a person, not a company — 'Hey, quick update' outperforms 'Dear valued customer'
- One clear call to action per email — not three links, not two buttons, one next step
- Use the customer's name — personalization increases open rates significantly
- Send at the right time — Tuesday through Thursday, late morning or early afternoon tends to perform best

Your email list is not just a marketing channel. It is your relationship with your most loyal customers. Treat it like one.

The Lesson

Social media builds awareness. Email builds revenue. The brand that owns its list owns its future.

Motivation

Start building your list on day one. Every subscriber is a customer relationship you own permanently. Protect it. Invest in it. Use it.

CHAPTER 79 — How to Handle Customer Complaints Like a Pro

Customer complaints are inevitable. No matter how good your product is, how clear your policies are, or how carefully you pack every order — something will go wrong at some point. A package will get lost. A size will run different than expected. A product will arrive with a defect. A customer will be unhappy for a reason you cannot fully control.

How you handle these moments defines your brand more than any campaign you will ever run. A customer who had a problem and had it resolved beautifully will be more loyal than a customer who never had a problem at all. That is not a theory. That is human psychology. People remember how you made them feel when things went wrong.

The Golden Rule of Customer Service

Respond fast. Respond with empathy. Resolve with generosity. In that order.

Fast does not mean perfect. A quick acknowledgment — 'I saw your message, I am looking into this right now' — is worth more than a perfect response that takes three days. Customers who feel ignored escalate. Customers who feel heard de-escalate. Speed of response is the first signal that you take your customer seriously.

The Four Types of Customer Complaints and How to Handle Each

Complaint Type	What They Need	How to Respond
Damaged or defective product	Replacement or refund, fast	Apologize immediately, ask for a photo, replace without friction
Order not received	Answers and resolution	Check tracking first, then contact carrier, keep customer updated every step
Wrong item received	Correct item, quickly	Apologize, send the correct item, let them keep the wrong one if feasible
Sizing or fit issue	Understanding and a fair solution	Acknowledge the issue, offer exchange or store credit, review your size chart

Complaint Type	What They Need	How to Respond
Unrealistic expectation	Clarity and empathy	Explain your policies calmly, reference where the information was available, offer what you can

What to Never Do

- Never argue with a customer publicly — you will always lose, even when you are right
- Never dismiss a complaint as the customer's fault — even if it is, your job is to resolve, not to win
- Never delay a response hoping the problem goes away — it never does, it only escalates
- Never offer a partial solution that feels like a fight — a generous resolution costs less than the brand damage of a bad review
- Never take it personally — a customer complaint is business feedback, not a personal attack

When a Complaint Goes Public

A negative review or social media post about your brand is not a crisis. It is an opportunity. How you respond publicly tells every person who reads that exchange exactly what kind of brand you are.

Respond publicly with the same generosity you would privately. Acknowledge the issue. Express genuine regret. Invite them to reach out directly to resolve it. Do not get defensive. Do not make excuses. Do not delete the comment — that makes it worse.

A brand that handles public criticism with grace and professionalism builds more trust with observers than a brand that never gets criticized at all. People know complaints happen. What they are watching for is how you respond.

Turning Complaints Into Loyalty

The best customer service outcome is not just resolving the complaint — it is creating a customer who becomes a brand advocate because of how you handled it. People share stories about exceptional service the same way they share stories about terrible service. Give them a story worth sharing.

Go beyond what they expected. Replace the item and include something extra. Offer a credit that covers more than the issue. Write a personal note. These gestures cost very little and create loyalty that no ad campaign can buy.

The Lesson

Your customer service is your brand's character made visible. Every complaint is a test. Pass it with generosity and speed.

Motivation

The customer who had a problem and had it resolved memorably will tell more people about your brand than the customer who never had a problem at all.

CHAPTER 80 — The Mental Health Side of Building a Brand

I am going to say something here that most business books will not say.

Building a brand is hard in ways that have nothing to do with manufacturing or marketing. It is hard in ways that live inside you — in the quiet moments between the launches, in the months when nothing seems to be working, in the comparison you make between where you are and where you think you should be. That weight is real. And pretending it does not exist does not make it lighter.

When I was building Engineered By Dré, I was a full-time student, working full-time, and building a brand at night. Most of my communication with manufacturers happened while the rest of the world was asleep. I was operating in isolation — doing things nobody around me fully understood, chasing a vision that had not proven itself yet, carrying the uncertainty of whether any of it would work.

That experience is not unique to me. It is the experience of almost every independent brand owner who has ever built something real. And it deserves to be talked about honestly.

The Things That Will Test You

- The comparison — watching other brands grow faster, get more attention, or reach milestones you have not reached yet
- The isolation — building something that the people closest to you may not fully understand or support
- The self-doubt — the voice that asks whether you are good enough, whether the brand is good enough, whether any of it is worth it
- The slow seasons — the weeks or months where momentum stalls and you cannot see the path forward clearly
- The identity question — when the brand struggles, it can feel like you are struggling. Learning to separate the two is one of the most important mental skills you will build
- The exhaustion — the kind that comes not from physical work but from carrying constant uncertainty

What Actually Helps

Community matters more than most people admit. Getting around other brand owners — people who understand the specific pressure of what you are doing — changes something. You realize you are not alone in the struggle. You gain perspective on your own journey. You find people who will push you forward instead of pulling you back toward comfort.

This is one of the reasons the chapter about getting around people who are doing better than you is not just business advice. It is mental health advice. The right environment does not just accelerate your growth — it sustains your belief when your own runs thin.

Rest is not weakness. A brand owner who runs themselves into the ground produces worse decisions, worse creative, and worse relationships — with their team, their manufacturers, and their customers. The most productive thing you can do on some days is stop. Sleep. Step back. Let the systems run without you for 24 hours. You will come back clearer.

Protect your personal life from the business. The business should serve your life — not replace it. If the brand is consuming every relationship, every hour, and every emotion you have — something is structurally wrong. Build the systems that give you back your time. Hire or outsource what you can. Create boundaries between work and the rest of your existence.

The Comparison Trap

Social media was designed to show you the highlights of everyone else's journey. You are watching someone else's launch day while you are in the middle of your slow season. You are seeing their sold-out notification while you are wondering why your ads are not converting. That comparison is not fair to you and it is not accurate.

What you are not seeing: the failed drops they do not post about. The manufacturer problems they did not share. The months where their revenue looked exactly like yours does right now. The doubt they felt in the same moments you are feeling it.

Your journey is not behind theirs. It is just different. And the obsession with their timeline will cost you yours.

When to Ask for Help

There is no medal for suffering in silence. If the weight of building becomes too heavy to carry alone — whether that is the business pressure, the financial stress, or the emotional toll — ask for help. Talk to someone you trust. Find a mentor who has been through it. Connect with other brand owners who understand. Seek professional support if you need it.

The strongest builders I know are not the ones who never struggled. They are the ones who recognized when they needed support and went and got it. That is not weakness. That is intelligence.

The Lesson

The brand you are building is a reflection of who you are becoming in the process. Protect the person building it. The business cannot outlast the builder.

Motivation

You are allowed to struggle and still be moving forward. You are allowed to rest and still be building. You are allowed to ask for help and still be strong. Take care of yourself. The brand needs you at your best.

CHAPTER 81 — Taxes, Write-Offs, and Keeping More of What You Make

Nobody starts a fashion brand excited about taxes. But the brand owners who understand their tax situation keep significantly more money than the ones who ignore it until April. This is not complicated information — it is just information that most people never get until they have already left money on the table.

I am not a tax professional and this chapter is not a substitute for working with one. What it is, is a starting point — the concepts and categories every brand owner should understand before they sit down with an accountant.

LLC vs S-Corp — When to Think About the Switch

You likely started as an LLC. That is the right move for most brand owners in the beginning — it is simple, flexible, and provides personal liability protection. But as your revenue grows, there is a point where electing S-Corp taxation can save you a significant amount of money.

Structure	How You're Taxed	Best For	When to Consider
Sole Proprietor	All profit as personal income — self-employment tax on everything	Testing an idea	Before you form an LLC
Single-Member LLC	Same as sole proprietor by default — all profit taxed as personal income	Early stage — under $50K profit	Starting out
LLC with S-Corp Election	Pay yourself a 'reasonable salary' — only salary subject to self-employment tax	Growing brands — $50K+ profit	When profit consistently exceeds $50K/year
C-Corp	Corporate tax rate — more complex, better for investors	Venture-backed or large scale	When taking on investors

The S-Corp election is one of the most commonly missed tax strategies for small business owners. Consult a CPA who works with small businesses to understand whether the timing is right for your specific situation.

Quarterly Taxes — Do Not Skip This

As a business owner, you are responsible for paying taxes quarterly — not just at year end. If you wait until April and have not been paying quarterly, you will owe a penalty on top of the taxes themselves. Set aside 25–30% of every dollar of profit into a separate account for taxes. Pay quarterly estimates in April, June, September, and January. This one habit will save you from one of the most common and preventable financial crises in small business.

Write-Offs Brand Owners Commonly Miss

A write-off (tax deduction) reduces your taxable income — which reduces how much tax you owe. Every legitimate business expense is a potential deduction. Here are the categories most brand owners either miss entirely or underuse:

Category	What Qualifies
Home office	The square footage of a dedicated workspace in your home — percentage of rent/mortgage, utilities, internet
Vehicle use	Miles driven for business — picking up supplies, attending pop-ups, going to the post office
Equipment	Cameras, computers, phones used for the business — often fully deductible in year of purchase
Software and subscriptions	Shopify, Klaviyo, Postscript, Canva, Adobe, Calendly, Zoom — all deductible
Inventory and manufacturing	Cost of goods sold — fabric, production, sampling, shipping from manufacturer
Marketing and advertising	Ad spend, photography, graphic design, influencer payments, event vendor fees
Education and books	Courses, books, conferences related to your business — including this book
Travel for business	Pop-up travel, trade shows, manufacturer visits — flights, hotels, meals at 50%
Professional services	Accountant, lawyer, consultant fees — all deductible
Business meals	50% deductible when the primary purpose is business discussion

The One Tool That Makes All of This Easier

Use accounting software from day one. QuickBooks, Wave (free), or FreshBooks. Connect it to your business bank account. Categorize every transaction. When tax season comes, your accountant will spend less time reconstructing your year — which means lower accounting fees and fewer missed deductions.

The difference between a brand owner who works with a CPA and one who does their own taxes without guidance is often thousands of dollars per year. Find a CPA who works specifically with small businesses or e-commerce brands. The investment pays for itself.

The Lesson

The money you keep is just as important as the money you make. Understanding your taxes is not optional — it is part of running a real business.

Motivation

Get a CPA. Pay quarterly. Track every expense. Keep more of what you earn. That money belongs back in the brand.

CHAPTER 82 — Write-Offs — How to Keep More of Every Dollar You Make

I bought a G-Wagon for the business. And before you think that is just a flex — it was one of the smartest financial decisions I made that year. Because I understood something most brand owners do not: the IRS allows you to deduct the full purchase price of a vehicle used for business purposes in the year you buy it. That deduction reduced my taxable income by the full cost of the vehicle. The government essentially subsidized a major purchase because I understood the rules.

That is what this chapter is about. Not just the basics — but the specific, real write-offs that brand owners in this industry can and should be using. The ones that require intentionality to capture. The ones that your competitors are leaving on the table because they either do not know they exist or do not keep the documentation to claim them.

This is not tax advice — work with a CPA who understands your business. This is education. Know what exists before you walk into that conversation.

Section 179 — The Vehicle Deduction That Changes the Math

Section 179 of the IRS tax code allows businesses to deduct the full purchase price of qualifying equipment and vehicles in the year of purchase rather than depreciating it over several years. For a vehicle used for business purposes, this is one of the most powerful deductions available.

For heavy vehicles — SUVs, trucks, and vans with a gross vehicle weight rating (GVWR) over 6,000 pounds — the Section 179 deduction limit is significantly higher than for standard passenger cars. Many popular SUVs qualify: the G-Wagon, Escalade,

Suburban, Navigator, Range Rover, and many others have GVWRs that push them into the heavy vehicle category.

Vehicle Type	Section 179 Limit (approximate)	Example
Standard passenger car	~$12,200 first year cap	Sedan, standard SUV under 6,000 lbs GVWR
Heavy SUV (6,001–14,000 lbs GVWR)	Up to ~$28,900	G-Wagon, Escalade, Suburban, Navigator
Pickup truck / cargo van (over 6,000 lbs, not SUV)	Up to full purchase price	Work truck, cargo van used for business
Fully electric or plug-in hybrid	Additional credits may apply	Check IRS Form 8936 for EV tax credits

The key requirement is business use percentage. If you use the vehicle 100% for business, you can deduct 100% of the allowable amount. If you use it 80% for business and 20% personally, you can deduct 80%. The IRS requires documentation — a mileage log that records date, destination, business purpose, and miles driven for every business trip.

This is not a loophole. This is the tax code working as designed — incentivizing business investment. A vehicle used to transport inventory, attend pop-ups, visit manufacturers, make supplier runs, travel to events, and conduct business operations qualifies. Keep the log. Work with your CPA. Claim what is yours.

Bonus Depreciation — Stacking on Top of Section 179

Bonus depreciation is a separate provision that allows you to deduct an additional percentage of qualifying assets in the year of purchase. In recent years this has been as high as 100%. As of 2024 it has begun phasing down but still applies to new and used property placed in service for business use.

Your CPA can help you determine whether to use Section 179, bonus depreciation, or a combination of both depending on your specific tax situation, income level, and state tax rules. The point is — both exist, both are significant, and both are missed by brand owners who do not have this conversation.

Every Business Expense Is a Potential Deduction — The Full List

Every dollar spent on the business reduces your taxable income by that dollar. The tax you save on that dollar depends on your tax bracket — but at a 25% effective rate, every $10,000 in legitimate deductions saves you $2,500 in taxes. At $100,000 in deductions, that is $25,000 back in your pocket. This is real money.

Category	What Qualifies — Be Specific
Photography	Every photographer you paid for product shoots, lookbooks, campaign content, pop-up documentation
Graphic design	Logo design, mockup creation, marketing assets, cover art, social media templates
Travel — Pop-ups & Events	Flights, hotels, Airbnb, rental cars, gas for every pop-up in another city — Sneakercon, Gotsole, ATL Streetwear Market, your own independent pop-ups
Travel — Manufacturer Visits	Any trip to visit a manufacturer, attend a trade show, or source materials
Vehicle	Mileage or actual expenses for business use — gas, insurance, maintenance proportional to business use %
Home office	Square footage of dedicated workspace as % of total home — rent/mortgage, utilities, internet, renter's insurance
Supplies & packaging	Poly bags, tissue paper, boxes, tape, shipping labels, hang tags, branded packaging
Shipping & postage	Every package you shipped — USPS, UPS, FedEx, DHL, Shopify Shipping labels
Inventory & COGS	Manufacturing costs, fabric, sampling, production deposits — the full cost of what you sold
Software & subscriptions	Shopify, Klaviyo, Postscript, Canva, Adobe Creative Cloud, Calendly, Zoom, Notion, accounting software
Advertising & marketing	Meta ads, TikTok ads, Google ads, influencer payments, ambassador commissions
Education & training	Books (including this one), courses, masterminds, coaching, consulting fees
Professional services	CPA fees, lawyer fees, consulting fees — all deductible in the year paid
Pop-up vendor fees	Every event registration, booth fee, or vendor application fee
Peerspace & venue rental	Every space you rented for an independent pop-up or production shoot

Category	What Qualifies — Be Specific
Meals — business purpose	50% of meals where business was discussed — client meetings, team meals, manufacturer dinners
Phone	% of your phone bill used for business — most brand owners use their phone heavily for business, claim it
Bank & payment fees	Shopify transaction fees, PayPal fees, Stripe fees, business bank account fees
Employees & contractors	Every payment to a photographer, designer, assistant, or 1099 contractor
Uniforms & branded apparel	Branded clothing worn at pop-ups or events that is not suitable for everyday personal wear

The Documentation Rule — If You Cannot Prove It, You Cannot Claim It

Every deduction must be documented. The IRS does not accept 'I think I spent about that much.' They accept receipts, invoices, bank statements, and mileage logs. The documentation requirement is simple but it requires a habit: save every receipt, categorize every expense, and keep records for at least three years.

- Use accounting software connected to your business bank account — Quickbooks, Wave, or FreshBooks
- Take a photo of every physical receipt immediately — apps like Expensify or your accounting software can do this
- Keep a mileage log for every business drive — apps like MileIQ automate this from your phone
- For travel, document the business purpose — a note in your calendar or receipts folder that says 'Sneakercon Chicago — vendor booth' is enough
- For meals, note who you were with and what was discussed — required for the 50% meal deduction
- Keep contracts and invoices for every photographer, designer, and contractor — and issue 1099s to any contractor you pay $600 or more in a year

The Meal and Entertainment Rules — What Changed

Prior to 2018, business entertainment — tickets to events, client entertainment, etc. — was 50% deductible. The Tax Cuts and Jobs Act of 2017 eliminated the entertainment deduction entirely. Business meals where food and beverages are purchased separately from entertainment are still 50% deductible. Know the difference.

- Taking a client or manufacturer to dinner — 50% deductible if business is discussed
- Buying tickets to a game and inviting a client — no longer deductible
- Catering at a pop-up event for customers — potentially fully deductible as a marketing expense
- Team meals where work is discussed — 50% deductible

The Real Opportunity — What This Means for Your Brand

Let me make this concrete. A brand doing $500,000 in revenue with $300,000 in cost of goods and operations already has $200,000 in gross profit. Now add intentional deductions:

Deduction Category	Estimated Annual Amount
Vehicle — Section 179 (G-Wagon example)	$50,000–$80,000+ in year of purchase
Home office	$6,000–$15,000 depending on space and rent
Travel — pop-ups, events, manufacturer trips	$10,000–$30,000
Photography and content creation	$5,000–$20,000
Software and subscriptions	$3,000–$8,000
Advertising	$20,000–$100,000+
Education, coaching, books	$2,000–$10,000
Professional services (CPA, lawyer)	$3,000–$8,000
Phone, supplies, packaging, shipping	$5,000–$15,000

Depending on your specific situation, intentional deduction strategy can reduce your taxable income by $50,000 to $200,000 or more in a year where you make a major purchase like a vehicle. The tax saved on that reduction — at even a 25% effective rate — is $12,500 to $50,000 staying in your business instead of going to the IRS.

That is not money you avoided paying illegally. That is money you kept legally by understanding what the tax code allows and documenting your business activity properly. This is what wealthy business operators do. Now you know how to do it too.

The Lesson

The G-Wagon was not a status symbol. It was a strategic business decision that reduced my taxable income by its full purchase price in the year I bought it. Understanding the tax code is part of building a real business.

Motivation

Work with a CPA who understands small business and e-commerce. Know what deductions exist before you walk into that meeting. The brand owner who understands their write-offs keeps tens of thousands of dollars more every year than the one who does not.

CHAPTER 83 — Funding, Working Capital & Building Without It

Money is the conversation most brand owners avoid until they are in a desperate situation — and by then the options available to them are limited and expensive. Understanding how to fund growth, when to use outside capital, and how to build a real brand using only what the business generates is one of the most important financial skills you can develop.

There are two paths every brand owner will walk at some point. The first is building with only what the business produces — bootstrapping. The second is using outside capital to accelerate what the business is already doing. Both have a place. Both have rules. And knowing which one applies to your situation right now can be the difference between smart growth and a debt problem.

Part 1 — Building Without Outside Funding

Most great brands started with nothing but the revenue they generated. Bootstrapping is not a limitation. It is a discipline. When the only money you have is the money the business makes, every decision gets filtered through a question that makes you a better operator: Is this the highest value use of this dollar right now?

That question — consistently answered honestly — is what builds financial strength. Bootstrapped brands tend to be leaner, more intentional, and more resilient than funded brands because they have never had the luxury of spending their way out of a problem.

The Bootstrapping Reinvestment System

The key to growing a brand on revenue alone is understanding the order in which to reinvest. Not all reinvestment is equal. Putting money back into the wrong area at the wrong stage slows growth instead of accelerating it.

Stage	Priority Reinvestment	Why
Just starting	Inventory of your best-selling product	Proven demand first — never reorder what hasn't sold
Early traction	Product quality improvement	Better product = better retention = less ad spend needed
Growing	Marketing and content creation	Once the product is proven, amplify it
Scaling	Systems and tools	Automation and infrastructure protect margin as volume grows

Stage	Priority Reinvestment	Why
Established	Team and delegation	Buy back your time to focus on vision and growth

The mistake most bootstrapped brand owners make is investing in marketing before the product and store are ready to convert. You pay for traffic that does not convert, waste the budget, and conclude that marketing does not work. It was not the marketing. It was the sequence.

Cash Flow Management When Bootstrapping

The biggest challenge in a bootstrapped fashion brand is timing. You pay for inventory weeks or months before you receive revenue from selling it. That gap — between when money goes out and when it comes in — is where most brands get into trouble.

- Never spend your next production budget on anything else — protect it like rent money
- Use preorders to fund production when you can — customers pay before you produce
- Build a cash reserve equal to at least one full production run before you start scaling ad spend
- Track your cash position weekly not monthly — problems become visible faster
- Negotiate payment terms with manufacturers — 30% deposit instead of 50% frees up working capital

The brand that manages cash flow well can scale on revenue alone indefinitely. The brand that ignores cash flow will hit a wall even when sales are strong — because the money coming in is already committed to the next cycle before it arrives.

Part 2 — Outside Funding — When It Makes Sense and When It Does Not

Outside capital is not a rescue. It is an accelerant. That distinction matters enormously. If your brand has a product problem, a conversion problem, or an operational problem — money will not fix any of those. It will just expose them faster at a larger scale. Capital amplifies what already exists. Make sure what exists is worth amplifying before you go looking for funding.

The right time for outside capital is when the business is already working — when product is selling, customers are returning, and the only constraint on growth is inventory volume or marketing spend. That is when capital accelerates a working system. That is when it makes sense.

Types of Funding Available to Brand Owners

Funding Type	How It Works	Best For	Watch Out For
Business Credit Card	Revolving credit up to a limit — pay back monthly	Small purchases, cash flow gaps, building credit history	High interest if you carry a balance — pay in full monthly
Business Line of Credit	Borrow up to a limit, pay interest only on what you use	Seasonal inventory purchases, flexible working capital	Requires established credit history and business revenue
SBA Loan (7a or Microloan)	Government-backed loans through banks — lower rates, longer terms	Major inventory investment, equipment, expansion	Slower approval process, requires documentation
Shopify Capital	Revenue-based advance — repaid as a % of daily sales	Inventory purchase when you have sales history on Shopify	Higher effective cost than a bank loan — read the terms
Clearco / Pipe	Revenue-based financing — advance on future revenue	Scaling paid ads, inventory for proven products	Only works when you have consistent revenue to advance against
Inventory Financing	Loan secured by your inventory as collateral	Large bulk orders when cash is tied up	Risk if inventory does not sell — inventory is the collateral
Friends and Family	Informal loans or equity from people who believe in you	Early stage when formal credit is not available	Define terms clearly in writing — protect the relationship
Angel Investment / Equity	Investor provides capital in exchange for ownership stake	High-growth brands with proven traction	You give up ownership — understand the implications fully

Revenue-Based Financing — The Most Practical Option for Growing Brands

For most independent fashion brands, revenue-based financing is the most accessible and practical form of outside capital. Tools like Shopify Capital, Clearco, and similar platforms advance you money based on your existing sales history and collect repayment as a percentage of daily revenue. When sales are high, repayment is higher. When sales are slow, repayment is lower. There is no fixed monthly payment that can hurt you in a slow season.

The key to using revenue-based financing correctly is knowing exactly what you are using the capital for and confirming that the return on that capital exceeds the cost. If you take a $20,000 advance at a 10% fee ($2,000) to buy inventory that generates

$40,000 in revenue, the math works. If you take that same advance and spend it on ads that do not convert, you have a $22,000 problem.

The Rules for Using Any Outside Capital

- Only use capital for things that directly generate revenue — inventory, proven ad channels, fulfillment infrastructure
- Never use borrowed money for operational expenses you cannot cover with revenue — that is a structural problem, not a capital problem
- Understand the total cost of the capital before you accept it — APR, fees, repayment terms
- Have a clear repayment plan before you borrow — know exactly how the revenue will cover the cost
- Start small — take the minimum amount you need, not the maximum you qualify for
- Build your business credit score deliberately — it unlocks better rates and higher limits over time

Building Business Credit From Day One

Most brand owners do not think about business credit until they need it — and by then it is too late. Business credit is built the same way personal credit is built: open accounts, use them responsibly, pay on time, and let the history accumulate.

- Open a business credit card as soon as your LLC is formed — use it for business expenses, pay it in full monthly
- Open a business bank account and maintain a consistent positive balance
- Get a DUNS number from Dun & Bradstreet — it is free and starts your business credit profile
- Pay every vendor, supplier, and subscription on time — some report to business credit bureaus
- As revenue grows, apply for a business line of credit — even if you do not need it yet, having it approved builds the relationship

The brand owner who has been building credit for two years when they need capital will have access to rates and amounts that a brand owner starting from zero cannot touch. Build it before you need it.

Shopify Capital & PayPal Capital — The Two I Use

I want to get specific here because I have personally used both of these and the experience matters more than the theory.

Shopify Capital and PayPal Capital are both revenue-based financing tools built directly into platforms you are already using. They do not require a credit check the way a traditional bank loan does. They do not require collateral. They do not have a fixed monthly payment that could hurt you in a slow month. Instead, they advance you money based on your sales history on their platform and collect repayment automatically as a percentage of your daily sales.

Shopify Capital

Shopify Capital offers eligible merchants a cash advance or a loan directly inside Shopify Admin. If your store has consistent sales history, Shopify will proactively offer you a capital amount. You can also apply directly through the Capital section of your dashboard.

Here is how it works in practice: Shopify advances you a lump sum — let's say $20,000. In exchange, you agree to repay a fixed total — let's say $21,800. That $1,800 is the cost of the capital. Repayment happens automatically as a fixed percentage of your daily Shopify sales until the total is paid back. There is no set timeline — if you have a slow month, less gets collected. If you have a strong month, more gets collected. The repayment adjusts to your revenue.

Shopify Capital — Key Details	What to Know
Eligibility	Based on your Shopify sales history — Shopify determines your offer
How to access	Shopify Admin → Capital section — offers appear when you qualify
Cost structure	Fixed total repayment — the difference between advance and repayment total is your fee
Repayment method	Automatic daily percentage of Shopify sales — adjusts with your revenue
No fixed monthly payment	Slow seasons do not create a cash flow crisis from repayment
Speed	Funds typically arrive within 2–5 business days of acceptance
Best use	Inventory purchases for proven products before a drop or busy season

What I use Shopify Capital for: inventory. Specifically, when I know a drop is coming and I need to fund a larger bulk order than my current cash position allows, Shopify Capital bridges that gap. The advance arrives fast, I place the order, the inventory sells, and the repayment happens automatically from the sales. When it is used for the right purpose — inventory that you know will move — it works exactly as it should.

What to watch for: the effective cost of Shopify Capital is higher than a traditional bank loan. You are paying for speed, convenience, and the fact that no credit check is required. Always calculate the actual annualized rate before accepting. For short-term inventory cycles where the return is clear, the cost is justified. For longer-term uses with uncertain return, it gets expensive.

PayPal Capital (Now PayPal Business Loan)

PayPal offers working capital to businesses that process payments through PayPal. Like Shopify Capital, it is based on your PayPal sales history and repaid as a percentage of your PayPal transactions. If you use PayPal as a payment processor on your store or for any wholesale invoicing, this is a tool worth knowing.

PayPal Capital — Key Details	What to Know
Eligibility	Based on PayPal sales history — minimum processing requirements apply
How to access	PayPal Business account → Working Capital section
Cost structure	Fixed fee based on advance amount, percentage chosen, and sales volume
Repayment method	Automatic percentage of every PayPal sale — no PayPal sale means no repayment that day
You choose the percentage	Higher % = faster repayment = lower fee. Lower % = slower repayment = higher fee
Speed	Funds typically arrive same day or next business day after approval
Best use	Short-term cash flow gaps, inventory, ad spend for proven campaigns

What I use PayPal Capital for: flexibility. Because repayment is tied specifically to PayPal transactions, it does not touch your other revenue streams. If you process both Shopify and PayPal payments, you can use Shopify Capital for one purpose and PayPal Capital for another simultaneously — and the repayments stay separate and do not compound against each other in the same channel.

The key advantage of PayPal Capital is the speed. Approval and funding can happen the same day. When an inventory opportunity appears — a manufacturer offering a better price for a larger order, a time-sensitive restock — PayPal Capital can move faster than almost any other funding source.

Using Both Together — How I Think About It

The way I think about Shopify Capital and PayPal Capital together is as two separate working capital tools for two separate purposes — and I make sure they never overlap in a way that strains cash flow.

- Shopify Capital — larger inventory orders tied to Shopify sales cycles. Repaid through Shopify revenue.
- PayPal Capital — smaller, faster needs or PayPal-specific cash flow gaps. Repaid through PayPal revenue.
- Neither is for operational expenses — both are strictly for inventory or revenue-generating activities
- I always know my total repayment obligations before accepting a new advance from either
- I calculate the effective cost against the projected return before accepting any offer

The mistake to avoid is stacking capital without understanding the combined repayment burden. If 15% of your Shopify sales are going to Shopify Capital repayment and 20% of your PayPal sales are going to PayPal Capital repayment simultaneously, you need to make sure your margins support that load. Run the numbers before you accept.

The Golden Rule for Both

Both Shopify Capital and PayPal Capital are tools. They are not income. Every dollar you accept is a dollar you owe back plus the fee. Use them for inventory that you are confident will sell. Use them when the math is clear — the revenue generated by the inventory will exceed the cost of the capital. When the math is clear, these tools are genuinely powerful. When the math is unclear, they are expensive debt.

The brands that use these tools well treat them like a short-term partnership with the platform — you borrow to grow, the growth repays the loan, and you come out ahead. The brands that use them poorly treat them like a paycheck — spending the advance on things that do not generate a return. Do not be the second brand.

The Honest Answer About Funding

Most brands do not need more money. They need better decisions with the money they already have. Before you look for outside capital, look at how current revenue is being used. Is every dollar working? Is the reinvestment sequence right? Is cash flow being managed intentionally?

If the answer to those questions is yes — and the business is growing but inventory constraints are the ceiling — then capital makes sense. If the answer to those questions is no — then more money will just accelerate the existing problems.

Build the discipline first. Then scale it with capital.

The Lesson

Capital does not fix broken systems. It amplifies existing ones. Build something worth investing in before you go looking for investment — including your own revenue reinvested intelligently.

Motivation

Whether you bootstrap or borrow — the rules are the same. Know what the money is for. Know what it costs. Know how it comes back. Never spend growth capital on anything that does not directly generate more than it costs.

CHAPTER 84 — Credit — Personal, Business, and Shopify Credit

Credit is one of the most misunderstood financial tools available to a brand owner. Most people think about it reactively — they need money, they check their credit, and then they either qualify for something or they do not. The brand owners who use credit strategically think about it the opposite way. They build credit before they need it so that when the opportunity comes, the access is already there.

There are three layers of credit worth understanding as a brand owner: your personal credit, your business credit, and platform-specific credit tools like Shopify Credit. Each one serves a different purpose and is built differently.

Personal Credit — Why It Still Matters for Your Business

When your business is new, your personal credit score is often the first thing a lender, landlord, or financing platform looks at. Your business has no credit history yet — so yours becomes the proxy. A strong personal credit score opens doors at the beginning of your brand's financial journey that nothing else can open.

Your personal credit score is determined by five factors:

Factor	Weight	What It Means for You
Payment history	35%	Pay every bill on time — this is the single most important factor
Credit utilization	30%	Keep balances below 30% of your credit limit — lower is better
Length of credit history	15%	Older accounts help — do not close old cards even if you do not use them
Credit mix	10%	Having different types of credit (card, loan, line) helps
New credit inquiries	10%	Every hard inquiry temporarily lowers your score — apply strategically

Target a personal credit score of 720 or above. At that level, you qualify for the best rates on personal guarantees, business loans that require personal credit checks, and real estate leases for pop-up spaces or warehouse locations. Below 680, your options narrow significantly and the cost of capital increases.

If your personal credit needs work, the fastest legitimate improvements come from paying down balances to below 30% utilization and making every payment on time for six consecutive months. There are no shortcuts that do not carry long-term risk — avoid credit repair companies that promise instant results.

Business Credit — Building a Separate Financial Identity for Your Brand

Business credit is completely separate from your personal credit. It lives in your business's name, under your business's EIN, and reported to business credit bureaus — primarily Dun & Bradstreet, Experian Business, and Equifax Business. A strong business credit profile allows you to access capital in the business's name without touching your personal credit at all.

Most brand owners never build business credit because nobody tells them it exists or how to start. Here is the exact process:

Step 1 — Establish Your Business Credit Foundation

- Form your LLC and get your EIN from IRS.gov — this is the foundation everything else builds on
- Open a dedicated business bank account — your business needs its own financial identity
- Get a DUNS number from Dun & Bradstreet at dnb.com — it is free and takes about 30 days to activate — this is your business credit ID
- Make sure your business address, phone number, and name are consistent everywhere — inconsistency confuses the credit bureaus
- Register with the Secretary of State in your state if you have not already — legitimacy matters to creditors

Step 2 — Open Your First Business Credit Accounts

Business credit is built by opening accounts in the business name and paying them consistently. Start with accounts that report to business credit bureaus — not all do.

- Business credit card — apply for one through your bank or through cards designed for new businesses (Brex, Ramp, or a bank-issued Visa/Mastercard in the business name)
- Net-30 vendor accounts — companies that extend net-30 terms to your business and report to Dun & Bradstreet are the fastest way to build a business credit profile. Start with vendors like Uline, Quill, or Grainger — they are known to report and approve new businesses
- Business bank line of credit — once you have 6–12 months of banking history, apply for a small line of credit at your business bank even if you do not need it yet

The goal in the first year is to have at least 3–5 active trade lines reporting positive payment history to the business credit bureaus. That is what creates a business credit score.

Step 3 — Use It and Pay It Right

Business credit is built the same way personal credit is built — use the accounts and pay them on time or early. Business credit bureaus reward early payment even more than personal credit bureaus do. Paying a net-30 account in 10 days creates a stronger positive mark than paying it on day 30.

Business Credit Score Range (Dun & Bradstreet PAYDEX)	What It Means
80–100	Low risk — best terms available, qualifies for most business financing
50–79	Medium risk — some financing available, may require personal guarantee
0–49	High risk — limited options, higher rates, often requires collateral

A PAYDEX score of 80 means you paid on time. A score of 100 means you paid early. Pay early whenever you can. It is one of the fastest ways to build a strong business credit profile.

Why Business Credit Changes Everything

Once your business has its own credit profile, you can access capital without a personal guarantee — meaning your personal assets are not on the line. You can lease warehouse space, equipment, and vehicles in the business name. You can open larger credit lines. You can apply for SBA loans with more favorable terms. You separate your personal financial life from your business financial life completely — which is the goal.

It takes 12–24 months to build a meaningful business credit profile from scratch. That is not a reason to wait. It is a reason to start today. Every month you delay is a month further from the access you will eventually want.

Shopify Credit — The Card Built for Your Store

Shopify Credit is a business credit card issued through Shopify that is specifically designed for merchants running stores on the platform. I use it and it has become one of my most practical financial tools because of how it is structured for the way a Shopify business actually operates.

Unlike a traditional credit card where you receive a statement and pay a minimum monthly payment, Shopify Credit works on an automatic repayment cycle tied directly to your Shopify revenue. Your balance is automatically paid from your Shopify payments on a regular basis — which means you are never accumulating interest the way you would on a traditional credit card if you forget to pay or carry a balance.

Shopify Credit — Key Details	What to Know
Eligibility	Available to Shopify merchants with qualifying sales history — offered inside Shopify Admin
How to access	Shopify Admin → Finances → Credit — offer appears when you qualify
Interest	No interest when balance is paid automatically through Shopify Payments
Rewards	Cashback on eligible Shopify spending — ads, apps, themes, shipping
Credit limit	Based on your Shopify store performance — grows as your store grows
Reporting	Reports to business credit bureaus — builds your business credit profile
Best use	Shopify ads, app subscriptions, Shopify Shipping, any Shopify ecosystem spend

What makes Shopify Credit particularly useful is the cashback on Shopify-specific spending. If you are spending money on Meta ads through Shopify, on app subscriptions, on shipping labels — you are earning back a percentage of that spend. Over the course of a year, that cashback is real money. And because repayment is automatic and tied to your revenue, the risk of carrying an interest-bearing balance is significantly lower than a traditional card.

I use Shopify Credit for all of my Shopify ecosystem expenses — apps, ads run through Shopify, shipping labels, any platform spending. It keeps those expenses separated from other business spending, earns cashback, and builds my business credit profile at the same time. Three benefits from one tool.

The Credit Stack — How to Think About All Three Together

The way I think about personal credit, business credit, and Shopify Credit together is as a layered system — each one serving a different purpose at a different stage.

Credit Type	Primary Purpose	When It Matters Most
Personal Credit	Gateway to early business financing — personal guarantee for first accounts	Brand new — first 1–2 years when business has no credit history
Business Credit	Long-term financial independence — access capital without personal guarantee	Growing — after 12–24 months of deliberate building

Credit Type	Primary Purpose	When It Matters Most
Shopify Credit	Operational efficiency — earn cashback on platform spending, build trade line	Ongoing — any time you are spending money inside the Shopify ecosystem

The goal over time is to reduce your dependence on personal credit and build a business that has its own financial identity and its own access to capital. Shopify Credit is a trade line that contributes to that business credit profile while also rewarding you for spending you were already going to make. Personal credit protects you at the start. Business credit liberates you as you grow.

Start building all three intentionally from the moment you form your LLC. The brand owner who has strong personal credit, an established business credit profile, and platform-specific tools like Shopify Credit has access to a completely different financial universe than the one who never thought about any of it.

The Lesson

Credit is not debt. Used correctly, it is access. Access to inventory when you need it. Access to capital when opportunity appears. Access to the tools that help you grow without draining the cash the business needs to operate.

Motivation

Build your personal credit. Build your business credit. Use platform tools like Shopify Credit for what they are designed for. The brand owner with strong credit does not scramble when opportunity comes. They execute.

CHAPTER 85 — Building a Team — Let People Do What They Are Great At

There will come a point in your brand's growth where the ceiling is not the product, the market, or the money. The ceiling is you. You are the bottleneck. Every decision runs through you. Every task requires your attention. Every problem waits for your solution. And no matter how talented you are, there are only 24 hours in a day and you can only do so many things well.

That is the moment when building a team stops being optional and becomes necessary. And the brand owners who navigate this transition well — who learn to identify the right people, put them in the right roles, and lead them effectively — are the ones whose brands continue to grow past that ceiling. The ones who cannot let go stay stuck under it.

The Fundamental Principle — Let People Do What They Are Great At

The biggest mistake brand owners make when building a team is trying to find people who can do everything. That person does not exist. The right approach is the opposite: find people who are exceptional at one specific thing and let them own it completely.

A photographer who is world-class at capturing your brand's aesthetic is worth more than a generalist who can photograph, edit, design, and write — but does none of them excellently. A customer service person who genuinely loves people and resolves problems with warmth and speed creates more brand loyalty than a distracted founder answering emails between everything else they are doing.

Your job as the founder is to do the things only you can do — the vision, the product direction, the brand identity, the key relationships, the strategic decisions. Everything else that can be done by someone else, should be. Not because you are above it. Because the business needs you focused on the things that no one else can do.

Founder's Work	Delegate or Outsource
Brand vision and direction	Customer service responses
Product concept and quality standards	Order fulfillment and packing
Key manufacturer relationships	Social media scheduling
Strategic partnerships and collaborations	Bookkeeping and expense categorization
Content direction and creative approval	Graphic design execution
Major financial decisions	Email flow management
Culture and team standards	Photography editing and retouching

Notice what is on the founder's side: vision, standards, relationships, decisions. Everything on the delegate side is execution. Execution is valuable — it is what makes the business run. But execution can be trained, documented, and handed off. Vision cannot.

Who to Hire First

Most brand owners hire in the wrong order — they bring on help for the tasks they hate before they bring on help for the tasks that are costing the business the most. Think about where your time is going right now. What are you spending hours on that is not the highest value use of your time? That is where to look first.

For most fashion brand owners in the growth phase, the right first hire is someone who handles the operational work — packing orders, managing customer service, maintaining inventory counts, handling returns. This is the work that consumes hours every week and requires almost none of the founder's unique skill set. Freeing that time up returns it to product development, content, and strategy — the things that actually grow the brand.

- First hire: operational support — fulfillment, customer service, inventory
- Second hire: creative support — photographer, editor, or content creator
- Third hire: marketing support — someone to manage ads, email flows, or social content

- Fourth hire: administrative support — bookkeeping, scheduling, vendor communication

Start with contractors and freelancers before full-time employees. The financial and legal commitment of a full-time hire is significant. A contractor gives you access to a skill set when you need it, at a cost you can scale up or down. As volume and consistency increase, the conversion to a part-time or full-time role makes sense.

How to Find the Right People

The best hires often come from your own community. The person who has been commenting on your posts for two years, who clearly understands the brand, who has shown genuine passion — that person is already aligned before the first conversation. Do not overlook them.

- Post the opportunity on your social channels first — your community knows your brand
- Ask other brand owners for referrals — someone who performed well for a brand like yours is likely to perform well for you
- Use platforms like Upwork or Fiverr for freelance creative work — test before you commit
- For local operational roles, job boards like Indeed or LinkedIn work well
- Look for people whose values align with the brand — skills can be trained, character cannot

How to Lead a Team

Leadership is not about giving orders. It is about creating an environment where people know exactly what is expected of them, have the tools to do it, feel valued for doing it well, and are held accountable when they do not.

The brand owner who micromanages every decision signals that they do not trust the people they hired. That creates anxiety, not performance. The brand owner who gives zero direction and expects results signals that they do not care enough to lead. Neither works. The sweet spot is clear expectations, appropriate autonomy, and consistent feedback.

The Four Things Every Team Member Needs

- Clarity — they need to know exactly what success looks like in their role. Not generally. Specifically. What does a good day look like? What are the standards? What are the non-negotiables?
- Tools — they need everything required to do the job well. The right software, the right access, the right information. A team member who cannot do their job because they lack the tools is a leadership failure, not a performance failure.
- Feedback — they need to hear what is working and what is not, consistently. Not just when something goes wrong. Regular check-ins, honest conversations, and genuine recognition when the work is excellent.

- Growth — they need to feel like being part of this brand is building something for them too. People who feel invested in the brand's success perform differently than people who feel like they are just filling a role.

Setting Standards Without Micromanaging

The way you protect quality without doing everything yourself is through documentation and standards. When the way things are done is written down — how orders are packed, how customer service is handled, what the photography brief looks like, what the brand voice sounds like — the quality can be maintained by anyone who follows the system.

Build the SOPs before you hire. Train to the SOPs. Trust the person to execute. Review the output. Give feedback. Refine the SOP if needed. That cycle — build, train, trust, review, refine — is how you maintain quality while freeing yourself from execution.

Your standards are only as strong as your willingness to hold them. If the work is not at the level you expect, say so — clearly, respectfully, and specifically. Tell them exactly what needs to change and what good looks like. Most performance problems are communication problems in disguise.

The Culture You Build Is the Brand You Become

The people on your team carry your brand into the world in every interaction they have — with customers, with manufacturers, with vendors, with the public. The standards you tolerate internally become the standards your customers experience externally.

Be the kind of leader you needed when you were starting out. Be honest. Be fair. Pay people well and on time. Acknowledge when something was done excellently. Have difficult conversations early rather than letting problems fester. Create an environment where people feel safe to bring problems to you instead of hiding them.

Your team is not just a resource. They are the infrastructure of the brand. Invest in them the same way you invest in your product. The return compounds.

The Lesson

You cannot build a great brand alone forever. The ceiling of a one-person operation is real. The brands that scale are the ones whose founders learned to lead, delegate, and trust — and build a team that carries the brand's standards as seriously as they do.

Motivation

Find people who are great at the things you are not. Let them own it. Lead with clarity and respect. Build a team that makes the brand bigger than any one person — including you.

CHAPTER 86 — How and When to Walk Away From Your 9-to-5

I built Engineered By Dré while I was a full-time student and working full-time. I graduated, started working as an engineer at General Motors, and continued building the brand alongside a demanding career. At some point the question that every founder with a job faces became unavoidable: when do I leave?

This chapter is for everyone who is building something real while holding down a job — whether that is a 9-to-5, a career, a trade, or any other source of income that is keeping the lights on while the brand grows. The question of when to leave is one of the most important decisions you will make. Getting it wrong in either direction has real consequences.

Leave too early and you put your income, your stability, and your brand under unnecessary financial pressure. Leave too late and the job becomes a ceiling that limits what the brand can become.

The Case for Staying — Why the Job Is Not the Enemy

The job is not holding you back. It is funding you forward. Every paycheck you receive while the brand is growing is capital that does not have to come from the business. It pays your rent so the brand does not have to. It covers your personal expenses so the brand's revenue can be reinvested instead of withdrawn. It removes the desperation that comes from needing the brand to survive before it is ready to support you.

Some of the best business decisions get made by founders who have a salary to fall back on. There is a clarity that comes from not needing every drop to succeed in order to eat. That clarity produces better decisions — longer-term thinking, more patient strategy, less panic when something does not work immediately.

Do not be in a rush to leave the job. Be in a rush to build the brand to the point where leaving is the obvious, financially sound decision — not an emotional leap of faith.

The Signs That You Are Ready

There is no single number that tells you when to leave. It is a combination of factors — financial, operational, and personal. Here are the indicators worth looking for:

Indicator	What It Tells You
Brand revenue consistently exceeds your salary	The business can replace your income — the financial foundation is there
Revenue has been consistent for 6–12 months	It is not a spike — it is a pattern. Patterns are what you can plan around
You have 3–6 months of personal expenses saved	You have a runway if the business has a slow season after you leave
The business has systems that run without you	You are not the only thing keeping it alive — it can operate while you build
Growth is being limited by your available time	The job is now the ceiling — the brand cannot grow past what you can give it after hours

Indicator	What It Tells You
You have a clear plan for what the first 90 days full-time looks like	You are not leaving to rest — you are leaving to execute a specific plan

Notice that none of those indicators are emotional. 'I hate my job' is not a reason to leave. 'I feel excited about the brand' is not a reason to leave. Feelings are real but they are not a financial plan. The decision to leave should be made on data, not on emotion.

The Number You Need to Hit

Before you leave your job, know your number. Your number is the monthly revenue the brand needs to generate — consistently — to cover your personal expenses, reinvest in the business, and give you a reasonable buffer for slow months.

Calculate it this way:

- Monthly personal expenses — rent, food, insurance, phone, transportation, everything you pay personally
- Add 30% for taxes — as a self-employed business owner you will pay self-employment tax on your income
- Add your monthly business operating expenses — software, ads, shipping, any overhead
- Add a buffer of 20–30% for slow months and unexpected costs

That total is your number. The brand needs to be generating that amount consistently — not occasionally, not in its best months — consistently before leaving the job is financially responsible.

If your personal expenses are $4,000 a month and your business operating costs are $3,000 a month, your baseline need is $7,000. Add 30% for taxes ($2,100) and a 25% buffer ($2,275) and your number is approximately $11,375 per month in consistent revenue. Know your number. Build to it. Then leave.

How to Leave — The Transition Plan

When the indicators are right and the number is hit, the transition still requires a plan. Leaving impulsively — even when the brand is ready — creates unnecessary disruption. Leaving strategically protects both your professional reputation and your brand's momentum.

- Give proper notice — two weeks minimum, four weeks preferred for senior roles. Your professional reputation follows you. Burning bridges at a job you are leaving is never worth it.
- Tie up loose ends — finish what you started, document what you know, leave the role in good shape. That is a reflection of your character, not just your courtesy.

- Do not announce it publicly until after you have left — announcing your departure before it happens creates awkwardness at the job and premature expectations from your audience
- Have your first 90 days planned — know exactly what you are doing with the time the job was taking. Content creation? Manufacturing development? Pop-up schedule? Have the plan before you leave.
- Revisit your budget immediately — without a salary coming in, personal spending discipline becomes critical. The business needs that capital more than lifestyle inflation does.

What Nobody Tells You About Going Full-Time

The freedom you imagined feels incredible for about two weeks. Then the reality of full accountability sets in. There is no paycheck coming on the 15th and the 30th regardless of what happened. There is no manager to blame when something goes wrong. There is no HR to escalate to. Every outcome — good and bad — is yours.

That accountability is powerful if you are ready for it. It clarifies priorities immediately. It sharpens decision-making. It makes you resourceful in ways that comfort never required you to be. But it can also be overwhelming for founders who were not emotionally prepared for the weight of it.

The transition is easier when:

- You already had systems running before you left — the business does not start from zero on day one
- You have a community of other founders who understand what you are going through
- You have a routine — the freedom of no schedule can quietly become unproductive without intentional structure
- You track your financials weekly — without a salary, knowing your numbers every week is non-negotiable

A Word on Timing From My Own Experience

I built this brand while being a full-time student and then a full-time engineer. I know what it means to build after hours. To communicate with manufacturers while the rest of the world sleeps. To carry the weight of a vision that has not proven itself yet while showing up to another obligation every day.

What I can tell you is this: the discipline you build while working and building at the same time becomes the foundation you stand on when you go full-time. The habits you create under constraint — the efficiency, the prioritization, the clarity about what actually matters — those habits do not disappear when you have more time. They compound.

Do not resent the job while you are still in it. Use it. Let it fund the vision. Let it teach you what it has to teach you. And when the brand is ready — when the numbers are right and the systems are running and the plan is clear — leave with gratitude and go build what you were meant to build.

The Lesson

The job is not the obstacle. It is the bridge. Cross it intentionally. Leave when the other side is ready to hold your weight — not before.

Motivation

Build the brand until it needs you full-time. Know your number. Hit it consistently. Then make the move. That is how you leave a job and never have to go back.

CHAPTER 87 — How to Come Back After a Bad Season

It will happen. A drop that does not land. A month where revenue is half of what it was before. A season where everything feels like it is moving backward. A moment where you look at the numbers and the brand and wonder if you lost the thing that made it work.

This chapter is for that moment.

First — what you are feeling is normal. Every brand that has lasted long enough has had a bad season. Not as an exception. As a part of the journey. The ones that survived it are not the ones who avoided the bad season. They are the ones who responded to it correctly.

Step 1 — Diagnose Before You React

The worst thing you can do in a bad season is make emotional decisions. Panic discounting. Completely rebranding. Abandoning a strategy that was working three months ago. Launching new products before understanding why the current ones are not moving. These reactions feel like action but they are usually noise.

Before you change anything, diagnose the actual problem. Pull your data.

- Is traffic down or is conversion down? — these are different problems with different solutions
- Did a specific product category slow down or is the whole store slow?
- Did anything change — a price increase, a shipping time change, a policy update, a drop in content frequency?
- What does your email open rate look like? Has your audience disengaged?
- What are your ads doing? Did a campaign stop performing? Did costs increase?
- Is this a brand problem or a market problem? — some seasons are slow for everyone in your category

The answer to those questions tells you what to fix. Without that diagnosis, you are guessing — and guessing in a bad season makes it worse.

Step 2 — Go Back to What You Know Works

In a bad season, this is not the time to experiment with new strategies, new platforms, or new product categories. This is the time to return to the fundamentals that built the brand in the first place. The product that always sells. The content format that always performs. The customer segment that always converts. The basics, executed excellently, will outperform a panicked pivot almost every time.

Step 3 — Reconnect With Your Customer

Bad seasons are often relationship problems in disguise. Somewhere the connection between the brand and the customer weakened. Maybe the content became less personal. Maybe the drops became less exciting. Maybe the brand started making decisions for the algorithm instead of for the community.

Go back to your most loyal customers. Email them directly. Ask what they want to see. Run a survey. Respond to every DM for a week. Show up personally in a way that reminds your audience that there is a real person behind the brand who cares about them. That reconnection will do more for a bad season than any ad campaign.

Step 4 — Use the Slow Period to Build

A bad season clears your calendar of the chaos that comes with a good one. Use that space. Fix the things you have been putting off. Develop the next product properly instead of rushing it. Audit the store. Build the email flows you never got around to. Work on your wholesale line sheet. Plan the pop-up you have been thinking about.

The brand that comes out of a bad season better prepared than it went in will always outperform the brand that just waited for things to get better on their own.

Step 5 — Protect Your Belief

The most dangerous casualty of a bad season is not revenue. It is belief. The moment you stop believing in what you are building, the decisions that follow reflect that. The content becomes half-hearted. The product development loses intention. The customer service loses warmth.

Protect your belief like a business asset — because it is one. Go back to why you started. Read the messages from customers who love what you make. Look at how far you have come from where you began. Bad seasons are temporary. The belief that gets you through them is what makes the next good season possible.

The Lesson

A bad season is not the end of the story. It is a chapter. How you respond to it determines what the next chapter looks like.

Motivation

Diagnose. Return to fundamentals. Reconnect with your customer. Build during the slow. Protect your belief. Come back stronger. That is the formula.

BUILDING UNDER PRESSURE

Execution when the stakes are high.

Nobody tells you about the 2 AM moments. The manufacturer that goes silent two weeks before your drop. The shipment stuck in customs. The product that looked perfect in the sample and arrived bulk with the stitching wrong. The week where nothing sells and you cannot figure out why.

Those moments are not signs that you chose the wrong path. They are the path. Every builder who has ever built anything real has had those moments. What separates the ones who made it from the ones who stopped is not talent. It is the decision to keep operating when it would be easier to quit.

This section is not about avoiding pressure. It is about performing inside it.

Don't Take Business Personally

One of the most important shifts I had to make was separating emotion from execution. I had to stop doing what André wanted and start doing what Engineered By Dré needed. Customers will complain. Manufacturers will disappoint you. Partners will fall short. A product you believed in will not sell the way you hoped. If you move emotionally, you will make short-term decisions that damage long-term outcomes.

When something goes wrong — and it will — your response time matters less than your response quality. Breathe. Assess. Decide. Move. Drama is expensive. Clarity is free.

The Four Responses to Pressure

Pressure Scenario	Wrong Response	Right Response
Product not selling	Panic discount immediately	Audit the trust stack — visuals, copy, pricing, policies
Manufacturer misses deadline	Blow up the relationship	Communicate clearly, document everything, find alternatives
A bad review goes public	Argue or ignore it	Respond professionally, fix the issue, learn from it
Sales slow down suddenly	Spend more on ads	Review data first — is it traffic, conversion, or product?
Copycat steals your design	Obsess over it	Protect legally if possible, then outrun them with quality

Consistency Builds Brand Identity

Brand identity is reinforced through repetition. Using the same photographers, models, and visual language builds familiarity and trust. Variety is fine. Consistency is essential. Recognition comes from repetition. When pressure is high, the instinct is to change everything. Most of the time, the answer is to do the fundamentals better.

Customer Service Is Sales

Customer service is not a support task. It is part of conversion. Clear policies, clear communication, clear expectations — legitimacy converts. Trust closes more sales than persuasion ever will. The way you handle a difficult customer interaction is marketing. People remember how you made them feel, especially when something went wrong and you made it right.

Copy Formulas, Not Products

Fashion has always had copycats. Do not copy designs. Copy systems. Study how brands scaled, how they marketed, how they structured operations. Formula beats imitation. Execution wins longer than originality alone. When someone copies your product, it means your product was worth copying. Let that fuel you, not distract you.

Personal Brand as Leverage

A strong personal brand amplifies the business. Supporting other brands, collaborations, and visibility expand reach and trust. People buy from people before they buy from logos. Visibility multiplies opportunity. Your story — your real story, not a highlight reel — is one of your most powerful sales tools. Share it.

The Days When It Does Not Feel Worth It

There will be days when you question whether this is the right thing to be doing. When the work feels thankless, the growth feels slow, and the gap between where you are and where you want to be feels too wide. Those days are not signs to quit. They are signs that you are in the middle of building something real.

The middle is the hardest part. The beginning has excitement. The end has proof. The middle has nothing but the decision to keep going. Most people leave in the middle. That is exactly why the ones who stay eventually win.

On those days, go back to why you started. Not the revenue goals. Not the metrics. The actual reason you decided this brand deserved to exist. Hold onto that. Let the systems carry the day. And wake up tomorrow and do it again.

The Final Operator Truth

Success is a revolving door. You must always be ready to adapt. Not every season is for growth. Sometimes survival is the goal. Pausing is not quitting. It is positioning. Control outlasts speed.

You are not building for today. You are building for consistency. Trends fade. Systems compound. Ownership lasts. Build something that still makes sense when the noise is gone.

The person who wins in this industry is not the most talented. It is not the most connected. It is not the most funded. It is the one who refused to stop. Refuse to stop.

CONCLUSION — THE LONG GAME

Adapt, stay aware, and keep moving forward.

This Was Never About Fashion

I need to say something clearly before you close this book.

This was never really about fashion. It was never about workshirts or hoodies or what GSM to request or how to find a manufacturer on Alibaba. Those things matter — but they are not the point.

The point is this: you have the ability to build something that belongs to you. Something that generates income, creates impact, and outlasts the years you put into it. Something that carries your name and your standards into the world. That is what this book was trying to help you reach.

Fashion was the vehicle. Ownership was the destination.

What This Book Actually Gave You

If you read every chapter, you now have something most people in this industry never get — a complete framework for building a brand that is designed to last. Not just to launch. Not just to trend. To last.

You have the mindset to start without permission and move without fear. You have the product knowledge to build something worth buying. You have the manufacturing understanding to control quality at scale. You have the marketing framework to turn attention into trust and trust into revenue. You have the financial literacy to protect what you build. You have the operator tools to make it run without burning yourself out. And you have the owner mindset to make decisions like the CEO of a real company — because that is what you are.

Nobody handed me any of this. I built it, made mistakes with it, rebuilt it, and refined it. Now it is yours. What you do with it is entirely up to you.

For the One Who Has Not Started Yet

If you have read this entire book and you still have not started — I want to talk directly to you for a moment.

You are not waiting for the right time. The right time does not exist. You are not waiting for more money. Most great brands started with less than you have right now. You are not waiting for more confidence. Confidence is built by doing, not by waiting to do.

What you are actually waiting for is permission. Permission to take yourself seriously. Permission to invest in your own vision. Permission to fail and still believe it was worth trying.

Consider this your permission.

You do not need a full plan. You do not need a flawless logo. You do not need a warehouse. You need one product you believe in, one customer who buys it, and the discipline to learn from what happens next. Everything in this book was built on that foundation.

Start today. Imperfectly. Messily. Uncertainly. Start.

For the One Who Is Already Building

If you are already in it — if you have a brand, customers, products, and you picked up this book looking for the thing that takes you to the next level — here is what I want to leave you with.

You already did the hardest part. Starting is the most underrated accomplishment in business. Most people never do it. You did. That matters.

Now the work is different. Now it is about refinement, not just momentum. It is about systems, not just hustle. It is about becoming the kind of owner who builds something that outlasts any single product, any single drop, any single season.

You are closer than you think. Every brand you admire was once exactly where you are — with the product working but the infrastructure still catching up. Keep building the infrastructure. Keep training your team. Keep investing in the foundation. The growth will follow.

The Principles That Never Change

No matter where you are in your journey — starting, building, or scaling — these are the principles that will always apply:

- Build the brand, not just the product
- Prepare for success before it arrives
- Move with confidence, not hope
- Use data to guide every decision
- Reinvest consistently and early
- Build systems that outlive you
- Scale when systems are ready — slow down when they need reinforcement
- Control your standards — your manufacturer will follow
- Protect what you build — legally, financially, and operationally
- Retain the customers you earn — they are more valuable than the ones you have not met yet
- Use every tool available, including AI, to build faster and smarter
- Stay in the relationship longer than the transaction
- The slow season is preparation — treat it that way

- Your name is the brand. Protect it in every decision you make.

The brands that last are not the loudest. They are not the most funded. They are not the ones with the most followers. They are the most consistent, the most aware, and the most committed to building something real over something fast.

Engineer your future. Do not hope for it.

The world needs what you are building. Go build it.

André Franklin

Engineered By Dré · engineeredbydre.com · Atlanta, GA

APPENDIX — THE 1-ON-1 CONSULTING FRAMEWORK

Four Calls. From Zero to Selling.

If you purchased the consulting option, this is the framework for our four calls together. If you are reading the book only, this section gives you the roadmap so you know exactly what each phase of building looks like.

Call	Phase	Focus	You Leave With
1	Foundation	Brand name, logo, LLC, Shopify setup, email & SMS tools	A real business entity and live store
2	Product	Design mockups, tech packs, manufacturer research, sampling begins	Active manufacturer communication started
3	Sample	Sample review, quality control, bulk order, rollout plan	Approved sample and launch timeline
4	Launch	Ads, private room launch, scaling systems, post-purchase flows	Revenue systems running from day one

CALL 1 — THE FOUNDATION

Brand Identity · Legal Setup · Shopify · Logo · Mindset

Call 1 is about building the base before building the product. This call covers brand vision, who the customer is, the Double R Method for naming, LLC formation, EIN setup, business banking, and a complete Shopify store with all five core policy pages. Klaviyo and Postscript are installed so the marketing infrastructure exists before the first product launches.

By the end of Call 1, you are operating as a real business — not an idea.

CALL 2 — THE PRODUCT

Design · Manufacturer Research · Tech Packs · Sampling Begins

Call 2 is where the product takes shape. This call covers mockup creation, tech pack fundamentals, manufacturer research on Alibaba (what to look for, what to avoid), the difference between China and Pakistan production, and how to communicate clearly enough that what you designed is actually what gets made.

By the end of Call 2, you have a product concept with design direction and have sent your first message to a manufacturer. The sampling process has begun.

CALL 3 — THE SAMPLE

Sample Review · Quality Control · Bulk Order · Rollout Planning

Call 3 is the quality gate. This call walks through how to review a sample — fabric weight, stitching, hardware, fit, branding placement. What to approve. What to send back. How to write a revision request that gets results. And how to transition from a sample into a bulk order with the right deposit structure, packaging decisions, and size distribution.

By the end of Call 3, you have either an approved sample and a bulk order in motion, or a precise revision request that protects quality. The rollout plan is built. The launch date is set.

CALL 4 — THE LAUNCH

Selling · Ads · Scaling · Long-Term Systems

Call 4 is the full system activation. This call covers the store final audit, the private room launch strategy (email and SMS first), Meta and TikTok ad setup, retargeting configuration, ambassador program structure, and post-purchase automation flows that keep revenue moving after the launch ends.

By the end of Call 4, the store is converting, ads are running, and the automated systems that build the business while you sleep are all live.

To book your 1-on-1 consulting session:

engineeredbydre.com

ABOUT THE AUTHOR

André Franklin

André Franklin was born and raised in Ypsilanti, Michigan. He studied engineering — moving through CAD, Civil, and ultimately graduating with a degree in Mechanical Engineering — before discovering that the same systems thinking that builds structures and machines can build brands.

In 2020 he relocated to Detroit, Michigan. In 2023, while working as a mechanical engineer at General Motors, he launched Engineered By Dré — a fashion brand built on the principle that great products are not hoped for, they are engineered. Operating from his home, then his garage, then a commercial warehouse, he scaled the brand from zero to over one million dollars in revenue in its first year and completed more than 30,000 orders worldwide.

Along the way, Engineered By Dré collaborated with the Detroit Pistons, Detroit Tigers, Detroit Red Wings, and Wingstop — and became recognized globally, even being copied by major fast fashion brands. The brand's workshirts, hoodies, denim, flannels, accessories, and home decor serve men, women, kids, and families across the world.

In 2026, André relocated to Atlanta, Georgia, continuing to build Engineered By Dré while expanding into consulting, education, and this book — his first.

ENGINEERED, NOT HOPED FOR. is the book he wished existed when he started. It is everything he learned, compressed into a framework that any brand owner — beginner or seasoned — can use to build something that lasts.

Find André online:

Website: engineeredbydre.com

Brand Instagram: @EngineeredByDre

Personal Instagram: @VeryOrganic_Dre

Second Brand: @UnseenGears

Email: shop@engineeredbydre.com

GET THE FULL EXPERIENCE

ENGINEERED, NOT HOPED FOR. is available in four options.

Tier	Price	What's Included
01 — Digital Ebook	$49	Full digital PDF · All 87 chapters · Build Checklist · Instant download
02 — Hard Copy + Ebook	$69	Printed First Edition 2026 + digital PDF + Build Checklist · Shipped to your door
03 — Full Resource Bundle	$150	Everything in Tier 2 (book + digital PDF + checklist) Mockup & Tech Pack templates — all clothing categories Tech Pack Manuscript — how to build & send a tech pack Editable SVG files — all 12 tech pack pages Manufacturer & Contact Directory — 95 vetted contacts
04 — Book + 1-on-1 Consulting	$1,000	Everything in Tier 3 · 4 calls with André Brand, manufacturing, sampling, and launch

Build Checklist included free with every tier — one page, every phase of building a drop.

If you purchased Tier 4 — read this book before your first call. Come prepared.

Previously purchased Tier 3? Your $150 is credited toward Tier 4 — you pay only $850.
Email shop@engineeredbydre.com with your order number.

---

engineeredbydre.com

Systems Over Hope. Ownership Over Attention.

www.ingramcontent.com/pod-product-compliance
Lightning Source LLC
LaVergne TN
LVHW071413210926
848486LV00004B/263